Magic Carpets,
Flying Ships,
and
Moonlit Kingdoms

The True Travel Stories of Marci Darling

Marci Darling

Magic Carpets, Flying Ships, and Moonlit Kingdoms

Copyright © 2021 – Marci Darling
All rights reserved.

Cover Art and Design @2021 Paul Dexter Inigo

Formatting by Rik: Wild Seas Formatting
(http://WildSeasFormatting.com)

Print: ISBN: 978-0-9981362-7-1
Ebook: ISBN: 978-0-9981362-8-8

Library of Congress Control Number: 2021909782

Praise for Miss Marci Darling

Fast paced and fun, *Martini Mystery* is a great read from Marci Darling, who shares my passion for burlesque, the circus, and New Orleans. It was a delight reading about so many places I've haunted in New Orleans.

> --Leslie Zemeckis, Bestselling Author of *Goddess of Love Incarnate: The Life and Times of Stripteuse Lili St. Cyr* and *Behind the Burly Q: The Story of Burlesque in America*

This is a tremendously fun, high-spirited read that is one part mystery, one part history of esoteric New Orleans history, and a couple of dashes of fashion. After a strange encounter at a nighttime parade, Darling takes readers on a wild trip through New Orleans secret societies and local lore in a dash to solve the mystery of a dead man, a mysterious key, an antique photograph, and a seemingly cursed Grace Kelly purse. She writes with wit and breeze and puts a smile on the reader's face, even when dastardly deeds are afoot.

> --Keith Allison, NYU Senior Editor, Author of *Cocktails & Capers: Cult Cinema, Cocktails, Crime, and Cool*

How can a book be both dark and mysterious yet imbued with fun and frivolity? *Martini Mystery* does just that, sweeping readers into an immersive and lushly evocative New Orleans adventure.

> --Michelle Finamore, Author of *Hollywood Before Glamour: Fashion in American Silent Film* and *Brioni*

Martini Mystery is a fabulous escapade into the glamour of New Orleans, its mysterious nightlife, costumes, and ominous undertones. A page-turning mystery that will also give you glittering giggles.

--Shannon Kirk, International Bestselling author of *Method 15/33, In the Vines, Gretchen, The Extraordinary Journey of Vivienne Marshall*

Martini Mystery is a fun read and perfect for a book club. You can serve food typical of New Orleans dishes along with the cocktails that were listed in the book.

--Megan O'Block, Bestselling Author of *Heart to Table, Diamonds and Dishes, Metamorphosis*

Author Marci Darling strikes a delightful balance with charming and provocative characters while providing a seriously suspenseful game of cat and mouse. With charming wit and dramatic flare, Darling dishes up opulence, cloak and dagger in one heaping serving. Martini Mystery is a captivating and truly satisfying first novel by Marci Darling.

--Leslie Martini, Author of *Matilda, the Algonquin Cat*

In Memory of my soul mate, Kim Murphy, AKA Rocket Sapphire, Lucky Murphy, and Empress Genevieve. If you were here right now, I would put a seashell crown on your head, a rainbow moonstone around your neck, and dance with you under the moonlight.

I can barely breathe without you.

To the girls who love traveling, the glittering globetrotters and happy wanderers who make their own magic.

And to Annabelle and Henry, my greatest adventure yet.

Table of Contents

Dear Darling Readers,

If I had five words of advice for my younger self, they would be Travel, My Darling! Make Magic!

Travel educated me, thrilled me, ignited and inspired me, healed me, and gave me a golden treasure chest of stories that keep me warm when it's cold outside. Traveling enriched my life in ways I never could have imagined. I worked and I saved and jumped into my next adventure.

When I turned fifty and my world exploded with loss, I turned to travel to heal. I planned an epic bucket list trip for me and my children to restore our shattered souls. The journey gave me the most priceless treasures of all: memories and stories with my beloveds. Instead of jewels, I keep my travel memories stored in a velvet box and I take them out whenever I need some sparkle.

And here they are for you, dear readers. I so hope you enjoy my stories, and when it comes time for you to make a decision, I hope you Travel, My Darling! Make Magic!

Backpacking Adventures
1990

Chanel No. 5 in Barcelona

Our first night backpacking as students, we took the train from Paris to Barcelona. I had spent six weeks in Paris on a study abroad with Santa Monica Community College in California, and I planned to backpack around Europe on my own. While at school, I learned two other students were also planning to backpack. Their names were Zar and Tanya, and they were expert planners. We didn't know each other, but we decided to start our backpacking adventures together.

I had a huge heavy Pendleton wool blanket rolled on top of my backpack, and the weight of it left burning marks on my shoulders as we trudged up and down curling stairs in Barcelona, trying to find a place to stay. This was before cell phones or Google, so finding a place to stay meant learning the address from a guidebook, walking to the place and knocking on the door to see if they had space. We quickly learned this is not the way to backpack. We decided two of us would stay with the packs, while one of us went and changed money and started calling places out of our travel books. Once we found a place with beds, we all went.

We finally found a place with three beds for us. We climbed the three sets of stairs to get to our room, where I took my pack off my shoulders and declared, "There is no way I'm carrying this thing around for six weeks!" I started to look for while the heaviest things to take away. The first thing to go was the heavy blanket on top. I donated it to the hostel and replaced it with a thin rolled-up straw tatami mat.

As I dug through my things, I pulled out the massive glass bottle of Chanel No. 5 I had packed. Zar and Tanya widened their eyes, "No!"

I nodded solemnly. "Yes, it has to go. It's too heavy."

We all looked at the bottle. They couldn't bear to see me throw it away, so we started dumping it on our backpacks and all our clothes. Our entire $4/a night room smelled of Chanel now. I threw the half-empty bottle in the trash.

Lighter now, we boarded the train to Nice, and as we rumbled along the ocean and the South of France, I stuck my head out the window, the warm wind whipping my hair, the starlight dancing on the ocean, and I screamed with freedom and delight. Several other backpackers stuck their heads out too and joined me in a frenzy of joyful screaming.

The next night, Tanya unzipped her pack and I saw my half empty Chanel bottle in her bag. I looked at her. She laughed, "I couldn't bear to throw it away." So now she was carrying it!

Still to this day, thirty years later, I smell Chanel no. 5 and I am transported back to that little room in Spain, to a time of freedom and lightness, starlight and ocean. Who needs a warm blanket and Chanel when she can have starlight dancing in her hair instead?

Barcelona

Sunflowers in Italy

Zar, Tanya, and I put om our backpacks and headed to Greece. As our train rambled through the countryside in Italy, we couldn't stop coughing from all the people smoking around us. We decided to get off at the next stop and run up to a different car together. I jostled off the train and started to trot to the front of the train, the weight of my backpack nearly knocking me over as it dug into my shoulders. That's when the train took off without me, and I realized my friends were not with me. I was alone. This was before cell phones, so if you got separated from your fellow travelers, there was no way to find them.

I was in a tiny Italian town straight out of a movie, with train workers playing cards around a table outside. They wore crisp blue uniforms and matching hats. They didn't speak English, and at that time, I didn't speak Italian, so I pantomimed my situation. I said, "Mi amigos! Ch-ch-ch (pretending to be a train) Arrivedercil!" (I waved here, then mimicked crying.) They thought I was hilarious. I kept pantomiming, they pantomimed back, neither of us understood what the other was saying, but we couldn't stop laughing. I finally shrugged, and when another train came along pointing the same direction as my train, I hopped on and hoped I'd find my friends.

As the train chugged along the Italian countryside, I looked out the window and saw a massive field of sunflowers, as far as the eye could see. It calmed me, and made me realize no matter where I landed, I'd be okay. I breathed and sat back in my seat, ready for whatever my next adventure would be. I arrived in Brindisi, a southern part of Italy where the ferries leave for Greece. It was very late, and as I walked through the train station with my pack, I heard familiar voices saying how worried they were about me. I turned a corner, and there were my friends lying in sleeping bags on the train station floor. They cheered when they saw me, leaping up, and hugging me, and ever since then, I have loved fields of sunflowers.

Greece

High Rollers in Monte Carlo

One warm summer night in Monte Carlo while backpacking, Zar, Tanya, and I decided to splurge on a banana split. We were eating on a cliff overlooking the sea. As backpackers, we never ordered dessert, because we had to save every penny.

But tonight, we were in Monte Carlo, and this was our way of being "high rollers."

The moon was hovering over the sea, turning the sky around it electric blue, and making the ice cream taste like we were eating moonlight itself. We ordered a second one, savoring the manna of cold cream with hot fudge drizzled over creamy bananas, all covered in a cream whipped into melt-in-your-mouth ecstasy.

We were so busy relishing the mix of flavors, we missed the last train back to our hotel in Nice.

Floating in the afterglow of our decadent indulgence of not just one, but *two* banana splits, we sat on the curb outside in the warm summer air, and leaned on each other. Watching the moon over the sea, we discussed possible solutions to getting back, involving things like speedboats, flying horses, and magic carpets.

Turns out that eating ice cream that tastes like moonlight softens the world. The jagged edges disappear for a moment, and everything becomes gentle and glowing.

It was in this soft world that three rambunctious Italian boys stopped to talk to us. They spoke very little English, but when they learned we were stuck, they offered to drive the three of us back to our hotel room in Nice in their convertible. It was technically in a different country, but only a thirty minute raucous drive back to our hotel. The ride was filled with loud singing, car dancing, and the kind of laughter that catapults into the air and cartwheels down the rocks before splashing in the sea. The boys dropped us back at our hotel, waved, and drove away singing.

Our hotel was the quirky backpacker-budget kind of hotel with a fat cat sitting on a rough piano in the tattered hallway, but that night, in our ice-cream-afterglow, it felt like the most luxurious five-star haven.

We quietly entered the hotel, shushing each other and giggling, until we collapsed into our beds. When my head sunk into my pillow, I looked out the big window and saw the moon sitting on a cloud, just like a cherry on whipped cream. I fell asleep feeling like the richest person in the world.

Important Business Trip to London...
Monkey Business!

I have always believed in one world, one love... I believe people should be able to go wherever they want to go, anytime they want, no matter where they were born or currently live. Did you know I was once almost sent home from London because they found my belly dance costumes and theater resumes in my suitcases? I don't love answering personal questions from strangers, so when the customs official started asking me why I was in London and where I was staying and how much money I had, I got a little triggered. When I'm triggered, I'm not my best self.

I was detained for hours, while the cute, but annoying, customs officials searched me and I made use of my extra time by practicing my headstands and cartwheels in the airport. So rude! I had no idea I wasn't allowed to work anywhere in the world. Obviously, if I had booked a job, I would have gone through the proper channels to work legally, but I'm not allowed to carry costumes and a resume with me?

In a hilarious twist, three weeks later, my best friend, Kim, came to join me and got the same customs officer!! He asked her who she was visiting and she mumbled, "My friend." He said, "Is your friend a belly dancer named Marci?" What are the chances? She had joked earlier that she would tell customs she was there on business and when they asked what kind she would say, "Monkey Business!"

In my mind, that monkey in charge of "business" is magical, a peddler of dreams with a music box and a tiny hat, transporting me to exotic lands.

Switzerland

The Time I Missed Running of the Bulls
(Because I was Brushing My Teeth in a Matador's Hotel Room)

I had always dreamed of traveling, and one day I saw a flyer at my community college for a Study Abroad in Paris. I worked five jobs: dance teacher, accountant (this didn't go very well–don't ask, I have blocked it out), movie theater ticket taker, assisting at a law office, and graveyard shifts at Canters Bakery to save enough money to go.

When I finally had saved enough money, I called my Dad to tell him, and though he worried about me and my fearless spirit, he said, "You did it, Kid!"

I wanted to be out exploring and not stuck with my nose in a book, so I read all the required books before we even left. That's how I learned that reading books that take place wherever you are traveling, enriches and enhances your experience. The first book I was assigned for my literature class? Hemingway's *The Sun Also Rises*, about a group of disillusioned young expatriates who travel from Paris to Pamplona, Spain, for the Running of the Bulls.

I was the opposite of disillusioned... I was "illusioned," enchanted by everything about traveling and living in Paris. I roamed the streets every day, soaking up the art, history, architecture, beauty and romance. I went to mass at Notre Dame, even though I'm not Catholic, and sat on an ancient bench, inhaling the incense and listening to the Latin chants. I ate brioche and eclairs for the first time, and joyfully splashed into fountains around the city at night. The world seemed marvelous, full of wonder, and I intended to not miss a thing.

Some of the other students and I decided it would be the best form of education if we followed the path of the characters of *The Sun Also Rises*. We bought tickets and boarded a train to Pamplona. I watched the French countryside pass by with fascination, with its charming farmhouses and beautiful fields, recording everything in my journal. We arrived in Pamplona and the chaotic cacophony of the city during the Festival of San Fermin. We sat in an outdoor cafe in the sunlight with cold drinks, watching groups of drunken revelers dressed in white, wearing red sashes, their arms around each other, weaving through the streets, singing. One would stumble, and they'd all end up on the ground where they'd stay, still singing, not missing a beat of their drunken songs. We made pillows out of our backpacks and slept in the park along with hundreds of other young students, and a group of six Norwegian boys with one guitar, who only knew the chorus of one song and sang it over and over... the song? "Let It Be." (Trust me when I say, that as beautiful a song as it is, you do not want to hear "Let It Be" on repeat for an entire night.)

The sprinklers came on at dawn and a hundred students, scrambling to get out of the path of the spray. We all dispersed in different directions, and I walked into the lobby of a hotel to find somewhere to brush my teeth and change my clothes. A handsome young man started talking to me in very limited English. When I explained I needed a place to change in my very limited Spanish, he allowed me to use his suite while he was talking to his "handlers." Turned out he was a matador, so I was truly living out Hemingway's ideal fantasy: in a hotel room with a matador. I was tempted to take a hot bath, but the matador started acting dodgy. I started to get suspicious of his motives when he told me that it's good luck to have sex before a bullfight. I thanked him for the use of his suite, and made my way back into the city.

It hadn't slowed down or stopped partying, even in the morning. I kept asking people what time the bulls were going to run, but they would just put their arms around me and sing louder, so I never got an answer. I figured if I stayed out in the streets with the crowds, I was sure to see the bulls. Hours passed, and it was time to return to the train station to head back to Paris. I met up with the other students and asked them why the bulls hadn't run. They said, "They did, first thing in the morning."

I had missed the Running of the Bulls because I was brushing my teeth in a matador's hotel room.

Oh well. I didn't get to see a bull, but I did see many drunk men pretending to be bulls, stampeding other men, who pretended to be matadors. Does that count? In my book it does. The people-watching was priceless, and so was the experience.

Kibbles and Bits in Paris

Someone once said to me that Paris is like a secret treasure that only opens itself to some people. Not everyone is touched in the same way by the magic of Paris. Personally, I find it hard to write about Paris. Why? I don't know.

Maybe the rich literary history that takes my breath away, walking the same streets as my literary icons, the souls who wrote the words that have enriched my life and changed my trajectory more than once: Anais Nin, Hemingway, Fitzgerald, Zelda, James Joyce, Gertrude Stein… so many.

Maybe it's the stunning artists that all lived in Paris, revolutionizing art over and over again. So many artists that have touched my life so deeply: Van Gogh, Toulouse Lautrec, Monet, Gauguin, Renoir, Degas…

And of course, the reverence for books, as evidenced by the long incredible history of my favorite bookshop in the world: Shakespeare and Co. Started by Sylvia Beach, the bookshop became a hub for all my favorite writers of the 20's, and she decided to single-handedly publish *Ulysses* by James Joyce, now considered one of the greatest books ever written. Like Proust wrote his tomes about eating one Madeleine, maybe I feel like Paris is such a deep and rich experience it would require me to write some big heavy tomes myself.

I had always dreamed of going to Paris. As a teenager, I would tear out the ads for Paris perfume to tape to my wall, which were usually big foldouts of pink roses with the Eiffel Tower in the background. No one in my family traveled internationally and no one I knew had ever been to Paris. One day while walking across campus, I saw a flyer for a Study Abroad in Paris, and that was it. I was going. The only problem? I didn't have the money. I worked five jobs for five months to save enough money to go, and once I entered the city, the enchantment began.

I loved Paris. Every time I turned a corner there was another stunning work of art, or some ornate gorgeous architecture that had been standing there for centuries. There was art everywhere, street performers, twirling colorful contemporary art mixed with centuries-old ornate buildings. No wonder Hemingway called it a moveable feast. Added to the transcendent art, I couldn't believe I was walking the same streets as so many of my literary heroes. I was only twenty, and just learning about my literary icons.

Here was a place that loved literature and art like I do, where the sidewalks and buildings literally drip with creative juices.

We were young students exploring a world we had only read about in books. We tripped across the top of the city like white foam on a cappuccino. We walked through the streets, kissed handsome young men, and jumped into fountains fully clothed. Everyone we met was enchanting and new, and it seemed every single one of them was from some exotic place.

I was a Mormon girl from Utah and I ended up becoming good friends with a Muslim girl, Zar, originally from Pakistan, but now living in LA. Zar and I didn't drink at the time, because of our religions, so we often ended up roaming the city together while everyone else explored the bars. One hot summer night, we were slowly walking near Hotel De Ville, and enjoying the multitude of handsome young men who stopped to talk to us. We decided to entertain ourselves by pretending to be different characters we created on the spot. The one rule, the character had to be part of a duo. So when a group of enthusiastic boys came up and asked us our names, we said we were Chabela and Rosarita from Mexico. (My Mother is Mexican and she used to call me Chabela as a nickname.) They believed us, and we were delighted when they called us by our fake names. The next group we met, we became Peaches and Cream, from Georgia, complete with southern accents. Then Maui and Kuaui from Hawaii, accompanied by a small hula dance, followed by Kibbles and Bits from Oklahoma. We laughed so hard when the cute boy in dreadlocks from Warsaw kept calling Zar "Beets" with his accent.

I don't know why we thought we were so funny, I just remember laughing so hard we ended up clutching each other to stay standing. We stood on a bridge over the Seine, snickering and watching the lights happily dance on the river. Like I said, froth on a cappuccino, whipped cream on a crepe… we didn't know anything, except that we were young and in Paris on a hot summer night, with merriment and twinkling lights all around us, and we deeply understood, on a soul level, what Hemingway meant when he said Paris is a moveable feast. It's been thirty years since that night, and the memory still feeds my soul.

Greece: Maybe Don't Drink Ouzo and Go Skinny Dipping? Or Actually... Do!

On our last night is Santorini, we were trying to stay up all night to catch our early morning ferry back to Italy. In the infinite wisdom of youth, we decided the best way to do this was to drink ouzo shots and dance all night. So eventually, we were so hot we took off our clothes and ran into the ocean, swimming under the stars with the crickets chirping all around us.

While swimming in water that felt like silk, we watched a massive ferry in the distance leave the island, and we shouted goodbye and waved at it, not realizing it was our ferry. We were completely out of money and we fell asleep on the beach until we were all bright red.

While we waited at the port that night, I was starving, so I pulled out my harmonica and played a hopping version of the only song I could play: *Amazing Grace*, while I danced around. The street vendors shook their heads, but did give me grilled corn as a gift for my musical talent, or maybe to get me to move along and stop hurting their ears with my one song.

We caught the night ferry and met some hilarious and handsome Greek students who spoke no English and we didn't speak Greek, but I showed them my tricks of balancing people on my feet and we were all rolling on the ground laughing even though we didn't understand each other verbally. We ended the evening in a massage train before we all fell asleep snuggled in a pile like a bunch of puppies.

It was the kind of adventure that happens when you drink too much ouzo and miss your ferry. This was one of the many backpacking experiences that taught me a life lesson that has served me well: stay open to the unexpected—sometimes the missed ferries are the best part of traveling.

Missed Meeting at the Eiffel Tower

While I was backpacking, I was joined here and there by my high school heartthrob, Erlend. He had been a foreign exchange student from Norway at my school in Utah, and we hit it off when we worked on the newspaper together. Tall and handsome, with blonde hair and teddy-bear brown eyes, Erlend left a trail of swooning hearts wherever he went. After he went back to Norway, we wrote letters to each other, and he came to visit me in Paris. When I headed to Greece, he headed to Norway and we made a plan: we would meet in three weeks underneath the Eiffel Tower at noon.

He was traveling, I was traveling, and there was no way to contact each other, so we had to make a plan and hope it all worked out.

I was having a wonderful time in Greece, but I was excited to meet up with Erlend back in Paris. On my way to the train station in Athens, it suddenly occurred to me that I needed Greek theater masks. Why theater masks? Because I was devoting my life to theater, and the masks were the symbol of my devotion. It seems crazy now, but back in 1990, you couldn't get Greek theater masks anywhere except Greece. What was even crazier was the pantomiming I had to do for the cabdriver to try to explain what I was looking for. I passed my hand over my face, making a happy expression followed by a tragic expression. It took him awhile, but he finally figured out what I was trying to say.

He drove me around from place to place, trying to find the comedy and tragedy masks, and we finally stopped at a museum and I was able to buy them in the gift shop.

My sudden quest took too long, and I was devastated when I missed my train to Paris. I hopped on the next fast train, the

TGV, but I was still six hours late to meet Erlend. I waited for an hour under the Eiffel Tower, hoping he would appear, but alas, no luck. There was no way for me to get in touch with him, so I had to just carry on without him.

A few hours later, I was walking across the street by the Hotel De Ville and who did I run into? There he was, crossing the street. I screamed and leaped on him, amazed at my luck. In this large city with all these people, I'd run into my one person. I was thrilled, but I did write a stern note to myself: do not decide it is imperative to buy something when you are rushing to catch a train.

In the end, for this one glorious moment, I had it all: theater, love, and freedom.

Paris Tattoo

Once I arrived on my Study Abroad in Paris in 1990, I wanted to get a tattoo on my ankle to celebrate my accomplishment. I pictured a future where people would ask me where I got my tattoo, and I would toss my hair in a nonchalant way and say, "Paris." This was before tattoos were common and before Google was invented. Tattoo parlors were difficult to find and located in undesirable locations. I looked in my dictionary, found the word for tattoo—"tatouage"—and asked around about where to find a tattoo parlor. Judging by people's reaction, you'd think I had asked if there was a store nearby I could rob.

I took the Metro to the crime-ridden red light district called Pigalle, and walked up a hill past prostitutes, pimps, and pickpockets to find Bruno's tatouage place. Full of drunk sailors, I looked out of place in my floral sundress with a bow in my hair, but I felt right at home. My Dad was in the Navy, and always a gentleman, so I adored sailors. However, when I told my Dad of my affection for sailors, he had a different reaction, a "Stay the hell away from sailors!" reaction.

I looked through the tattoo books to get ideas for a tattoo, and when I came across a *marguerite* – daisy, I knew I'd found the right one. Seeing daisies always made me feel joyful. I showed it to Bruno, who was wearing a white lab coat. He shook his head, pushing me out the door and pantomiming eating. I turned around and looked at him as he flipped his sign from open to closed. Rude.

I went to the parlor over and over, and Bruno kept refusing to give me a tattoo of the daisy on my ankle. Everyone spoke in French and I sat on a chair and happily watched a wide array of fascinating people getting tattoos. After my third visit, Bruno pinched his fingers at me, saying, "Ahhh, douleur dans le cul!" All the men in the joint looked at me, laughing. I smiled and blushed, assuming Bruno's term of affection for me meant something like, "Most beautiful girl I've ever seen!" or "Magical girl who's going places!" I asked one of the men what the phrase meant. He consulted with the others and managed to say, "Pain in ze… what you call it? … ass. Yes, pain in ze ass."

I put my hands on my hips and sighed. "Thanks Bruno. Now, I'd like my tattoo." He reluctantly gave me the daisy tattoo on my ankle, and he must have had trouble seeing over his gray moustache because it turned out completely lopsided. I had to call it a "Wild Daisy" to explain its haphazard shape. Eight years later, I returned to Bruno's Tatouage and had the daisy covered with a tattoo of the black cat from "Le Chat Noir" by Toulouse Lautrec. An adorable young tattoo artist did it. I showed him a photo of "Le Chat Noir", and when he started adding extra lines, I said, "What are you doing?" He said, "Arteestic License!" Why did I insist on getting tattoos at Bruno's? I don't know.

I was getting the cat done when Bruno when entered the joint. I said, "Hi Bruno. Remember me?" He laughed and shook his head and said, "Douleur dans le cul." I'm glad I'm so memorable.

An Unusual Summer Romance

I met him on a rainy summer night in Paris, the kind of night that's made for kissing. Chris was English, with thick wavy black hair, warm eyes, and an accent that could melt butter in a freezer. In my journal at the time, I described our meeting as, "I met a gorgeous, we are talking stunning, British guy." By the end of our first evening together, he put his arms around me while we were waiting for a taxi and I turned around and kissed him. By the next day, we were officially "dating," and we spent much of our time that summer staring into each other's eyes and kissing on every street corner. It was the kind of passionate summer love where you go to the pub and ask for a dark booth in the back so you can wrap around each other and kiss until you are seeing stars. We gallivanted around Paris together nearly every day, when he wasn't working of course.

Chris had an unusual job with unusual hours. He was an artist at a museum, but not the quiet-reverential-priceless-art kind of museum. He worked at the Museum of Horror and Torture. He was the artist who worked on the wax dummies, painting their eyes and lips sewn shut, or sculpting their faces into expressions of pain and terror as their wax fingernails were pulled out by some executioner. Aaarrrggghhh. The Museum of Horror and Torture was a pop-up museum debuting in 1990, and as I knew nothing about torture, I never asked him what exactly he was painting. But then there came the day when he invited me and my friends to come see the exhibits, and let's just say I'm still haunted. It was like passing a car crash: you don't want to look but you can't help it. Now you might think that Chris was a strange bird with a job like that, but he wasn't. He was just a kind artist who happened to be working on that particular museum for a few months.

Chris liked to have a few pints every night after work, and honestly, if I spent my days creating torture scenes, I would probably need a hundred pints every evening. Even though I didn't drink at the time, I still loved going to taverns for the people-watching. Throw in some steamy kissing and I'm a happy barfly. I loved hearing the stories of the other patrons, reading the poetry on the wall, the charm of the fat cat sitting on its own barstool at the bar like it was just about to order a whisky.

One night, I took Chris to my favorite haunt, La Caveau de la Huchette, in St. Michel. Ironically, the Caveau de la Huchette was once a medieval torture chamber back in the 1400's, but in a recent century, it had been turned into a swing-dancing club. I shivered when I saw the metal hooks on the walls, and imagined how many screams those stone walls had heard over the centuries... that damn Museum of Torture had put images in my mind I couldn't erase. But if anything can wash away pain and suffering, it's music and dancing. The stone walls seemed to thump with the energy of the crowded room, with dancers rising up and down in one sweaty mass, occasionally separating when one couple started throwing each other into the air, and the entire crowd cheered and danced harder, bigger, brighter, like shooting stars that didn't want their light to end.

But as we all know, all wonderful things must come to an end. After a few weeks of our passionate Parisian romance, Chris's job ended and he went back to England. I kissed him goodbye but I wasn't too sad, because I happened to be deeply involved with a new kind of torture, the kind of sweet torture that happens when you fall in love with a city. When I walked across the bridges in Paris at night, and stopped to watch the lights glimmer on the Seine, my heart ached with the beauty. I felt the same divine ache when I bit into a warm banana nutella crepe bought from the street vendor while watching children play with the sailboats in Luxembourg Park; or when I listened to poetry read aloud by raspy voices at midnight by candlelight in a bookshop across from Notre Dame; or when I ended up splashing in a fountain on a warm rainy night; the sweet torture of summertime in Paris.

Bad Hair Day in Belgium

Doing my hair while traveling has always been challenging. When backpacking, it was even harder. It was impossible to fit hair paraphernalia inside an overstuffed pack, and even if you were able to fit a hair dryer into your bag, there were no plugs in the hostels. This led me to the awesome idea of occasionally sleeping in sponge curlers. I'm not sure why I thought this was a good idea, except in my mind, I now had beautiful curls, although in reality it looked more like I skipped the blow dryer and stuck my finger in the electric socket. Whenever I sponge-curled my hair back home, my Dad would ask me if the cat had done my hair. If my Dad had seen my hair the day I was in Belgium, he would have asked me if I had met a group of alley cats and let them do my hair. It was sticking out in ringlet curls in every direction.

So, a few years ago I went to Paris with an adapter and immediately attempted to curl my hair before going out. I was staying at L'Hotel, and the light in the bathroom was so dim I could barely see the smoke rising off my hair, but I did smell the burnt hair wafting around the room. I gave up on curling it, and an hour later, I was having the most amazing crepes in my life at Little Breizh, when I touched my hair and a big chunk of my burnt hair fell to the floor. I touched it again in disbelief and another chunk came out in my hand. I ended up buying a dashing beret and wearing it around the city, which doubled up as a head-warmer and hair-cover.

I have finally learned my lesson. I now travel with hats, feathers, flowers, and cute ponytails that I clip in for evenings out, giving myself and all who encounter me the illusion that my hair is cooperating that day. And who doesn't love a good illusion?

Mozart and the Galloping Pianos of Salzburg

As a backpacker, we would save money on hotels by taking overnight trains. Arriving in countries in the wee hours of the morning meant sitting in a park with our backpacking, waiting for the cities to open. Tanya and I arrived in Salzburg at dawn and stepped outside the train station, the mountains soaring around us, the smell of baking bread leading us to a little gingerbread-house-shaped-bakery. The aroma of a warm loaf of bread fresh out of the oven, makes me feel like I'm floating, and I can't even remember my feet touching the sidewalk that morning as I followed the wafting scent. In an effort to save money, we bought one loaf of dark bread that weighed more than Tanya. We tore off pieces all morning, sharing it with everyone we met, but maybe it was magic bread because it never seemed to get smaller.

Why did we choose to trek to Salzburg? One word: Mozart. I loved Mozart, and I wanted to see where he was born and where he grew up. I wanted to breathe the same air that had nourished this genius, who had enriched my life in so many ways.

I walked reverently through his house like I was in a church. When I saw his piano with its delicate wood, and imagined his fingers on the keys, I wanted to cry. I couldn't believe that I was looking at his actual piano, the one where he wrote music that actually changed people's lives.

Mozart began composing at the age of five. Five! Can you imagine a boy sitting at the piano and writing a minuet when his feet didn't even touch the floor? He wrote his first opera at the age of 14.

His handwritten sheet music was on display in glass cases. I stared at the sheets for a long time, imagining his hand holding a pen and writing such beautiful music. The notes looked like their own language, like a message from an ancient civilization giving out a secret code for euphoria. When I walked outside his house, I sat down on the steps to take in everything I had just seen.

I looked at the stone steps beneath me and wondered if he ever sat down right here and listened to the birds sing? Did he eat his own loaf of black bread while inhaling the pine trees and watching the light change?

Or was it hard for him to sit down and listen to birds when music was stampeding through his head like wild pianos let loose in the mountains? If he was writing symphonies and operas as a child, I wonder what it was like inside his mind? Was it lush and gorgeous, like the music, or did it get chaotic in there until it got out of his head and onto the page?

I like to imagine the mountains around his home filled with wild stampeding pianos.

Tanya came and sat next to me on the steps and I told her my vision of pianos, galloping around the mountains, breathless, wild, and glorious. I told her I had heard that if you give them a warm loaf of bread, it calms them so they will sit still and you can play the most enchanting music. She looked at me out of the corner of her eye, like she does when she's not sure if I've truly lost my mind or just making up another story. She laughed and laid her head on my shoulder and together we watched the sunlight on the leaves, smelling the fireplaces and crisp autumn air.

Now I can't stop thinking of the wild pianos of Salzburg, and in my dreams, they gallop around the mountains, breathless and wild and glorious. If you catch one, you can sit down and make music like Mozart.

A Passion Play in Oberammergau

When I told my high school best friend, Matt, that I was going backpacking, he said I absolutely MUST go to a charming town in the Bavarian Alps called Oberammergau. He said the historic town put on a passion play once every ten years, and it was happening in 1990. Now I wasn't exactly sure what a Passion Play was, but I like passion and I like plays, so I decided I must go. There was no way to know if it was actually happening, or if we could even get tickets, as there was no internet.

I eventually learned that the Passion Play began in 1633. The people of the town had been suffering from the Plague for months, and after dozens of deaths, they made a pledge that they would act out a Passion Play about suffering, death, and resurrection every ten years, and the legend says after the pledge, there wasn't another death from the Plague.

So if you're looking for something to do in 2022, guess what's playing in Oberammergau?

So back to 1990, Tanya and I made it our mission to get to Oberammergau. We rode a bus for hours and hours through the most enchanting forests and mountains I've ever seen, and that's saying something since I grew up in the mountains. Picturesque cows dotted the hillsides wearing huge bells around their necks, their big gentle eyes slowly chewing their grass as they watched the bus pass. We climbed higher and higher, the air smelling fresher and crisper, until we finally arrived in the tiny Bavarian town.

It smelled like home, with the lush forests covering the mountains, the smell of evergreen, wildflowers and even that touch of snow that stays on the highest peak, even in the middle of summer.

And it looked like a fairy tale town. If you imagine an elaborate gingerbread village, that is Oberammergau. Think colorful paintings on the outside of buildings, curving doorways, swooping steeples, bright window shutters and boxes spilling flowers... This is a place where some people still wear Lederhosen, feathered caps, and dirndls. It's also renowned for its wood carving, and we all know woodcarvers are right at home in fairy tales.

There's even a house called the "Hansel and Gretel House" with scenes from the fairy tale painted all over the outside. And across the street sits the "Little Red Riding Hood House" with scenes from that fairy tale painted on it.

In the center of the town was a church, and the entire area around it was packed with people who had also come for the once-a-decade Passion Play.

We couldn't get in.

We had taken the long journey to Oberammergau and we couldn't fit in the church. We sat outside in the square and hoped that we would get a little of the legendary magic by osmosis. The sun set and the stars appeared, and we finally decided we should find a place to sleep. We went to the local hostel, but I didn't want to spend the money. We made a plan that Tanya would get a bed and then she'd sneak me in through a window and we'd share a bed.

Once I was outside, however, I decided I wanted to sleep by the river. The smell of the pine trees and the mossy stones of the river, the lulling hush of tumbling water, the blanket of stars... it all felt like home. The temperature dropped in the night, and my blanket made of starlight wasn't quite warm enough. I pulled some clothes out of my backpack to pile on top of me for warmth. It seems I should have been worried about hungry wild animals, but I didn't. I felt safe, and happy, and actually this turned out to be the best night of sleep I had the entire time I was backpacking. I remember waking up in the morning to the sound of chirping birds, the tinkling rush of the river, the sun shooting golden rays through trees and thinking, am I home? I looked around, touched my heart and sighed.. Yes I was.

Prague

Prague: The Wall Came Down

It was 1990. The wall had just fallen. The Czech Republic was still called Czechoslvakia. The city was like a cauldron bubbling over with hope and possibility. You could feel the electricity in the air. In the middle of the square, a military tank lay flipped over on its side, with flowers and peace signs and the words "Love Makes the World Go Round" on the side. There were no cell phones or internet, and I spent my days roaming the cobblestone streets, gazing in wide-eyed wonder at a world full of marvelous things. I felt like I was made of stardust and joy and magical moments and even now, after all the loss, I still feel that way.

Ecoute in Paris

If you walk near St. Eustache Cathedral in Paris, you will see an enormous stone sculpture of a large head leaning sideways with a massive stone hand cupping its ear. When I went to school in Paris in 1990, I liked to climb on it and pretend the giant hand was carrying me away. It became a meeting place for all of us in between hanging out at the nearby James Joyce Bar and school events: "Meet me at the giant head."

Nearly a decade later, I returned to "the head" with my best friend, Kim. Again, we climbed all over the hand, draping ourselves across it, pretending it was grabbing us and carrying us away somewhere magical. For our final photo, we straddled the hand and held each other, her cheek warm on mine, a treasured moment. Then we jumped down and continued walking through Les Halles where I found a white fringe flapper dress for $20, which I took as a sign of good luck. I wore that dress for years. It was my sassy fringe flapper dress, and when I twisted and shimmied, the fringe flew out in all directions. When people would say, "I love your dress, where did you get it?" I could sound epically glamorous. "Oh I picked it up in a little shop in Paris."

Twenty years after my visit with Kim, I returned to "the head" with my teenage children. While they climbed all over the hand, I sat down in its palm and let it hold me in all my broken-hearted sadness.

Kim was gone now, the demons of her mental illness finally captured her and took her away forever. I had married my true love, but eventually learned he was not true, and my marriage had exploded into a raging inferno that quickly burnt my life to the ground. I now had children of my own, gorgeous and shining, my heart intertwined with theirs.

I turned my head and watched my daughter scream that she was falling, and my son ran and caught her foot in his hands and pushed her back up on top of the head. Even as teenagers, they still liked to play make-believe. They were growing up and would soon be on their own adventures.

I sat quietly in the giant hand, the stone warmed by the sun, and listened to my heartbeat among the children shouting and laughing in different languages around me.

I thought about the 20-year-old me who had been full of childlike wonder and adventure and enchanted by everything about Paris and living out my dream of visiting such a magnificent city.

I thought about 28-year-old me climbing the hand with my soul mate and best friend, wrapping our arms around each other, feeling like we would be intertwined forever… one glorious treasured moment caught on camera. I didn't know then that it wouldn't last forever.

And here I was, 50-year-old me, letting the hand gently hold me.

I wonder if the artist who created the sculpture, Henry de Miller, knew how many broken hearts and singing hearts his sculpture would hole?

All these years climbing on it, and I had never known its actual name was "Ecoute." It means, "listen" in French. And I guess if you have one word to share with the world, "listen" is a good one.

A Remote Forest in Norway

My trip to Norway to see my lover in March of 1991 ended up very different than I had pictured.

I arrived in Oslo for two weeks of romance in the deep winter. Of course my gorgeous Norwegian lover immediately booked the lead role in his university play and started all-day rehearsals, leaving me on my own. Because I love children and I always need money, I decided to spend my days working at a nearby childcare owned by his friend. Every day of my two-week visit, I bundled up in a wool sweater and puffy coat and headed out into the cold dark morning to walk to the preschool. The Norwegian babies arrived with their rosy cheeks and bright eyes, layered in at least five different sets of clothing. We played games, sang songs, snacked, then stacked them in baby buggies and pushed them around the island for fresh air.

My jet lag was overpowering. I would work all day, have dinner, and fall asleep till midnight, when I would spring to life. I read all 840 pages of *Brothers Karamazov* by Dostoyevsky on this trip, which ended up changing my life, so it was an excellent use of my time. I guess I didn't need to go all the way to Norway to read a book, but that's exactly what I did. I barely saw my lover, but I did learn three very important Norwegian phrases: "ikke spis:" (*don't eat that*) "ikke bit" (*don't bite*) and "jeg elska deg (*I love you*). And really, those phrases cover nearly any situation.

On the last weekend, my lover, his friends, and I all piled into a small car and drove several hours up to a remote part of Northern Norway. The guys were speaking Norwegian the entire time, and playing Leonard Cohen on the stereo, so I spent the trip looking out the window at the little fairy-tale houses with lit-up windows and smoke coming out of their chimneys. I like to imagine the people inside the houses and make up stories about what they are doing. Are they dancing around their kitchen, making dinner for the children? Or did they just have a fight and they aren't speaking to each other? Are they sitting by the fire reading, or sitting down to play the piano?

We were nearly out of gas and all the stations were closed, so we pulled into one, put the nozzle into the car and the guys jumped up and down on the hose to try to get the last bits of gas out of it. We continued deeper into the woods. Finally stopping in the middle of some trees. It was dark in this part of Norway, the sky lit only by crisp starlight. Two guys pulled cross-country skis off the top of the car and strapped them on to their shoes. They disappeared into the woods with a flashlight. The other four of us sat in the car, huddled together for warmth, as we couldn't turn on the car due to our lack of gas. The guys eventually came back carrying a few more pairs of skis. There wasn't enough for me, so I had to ride on someone's back through the forest to get to the cabin.

So now, it was 2am in the middle of a remote forest in Norway, with snow so deep it could swallow me whole, and I'm riding on the back of a young man, surrounded by thick pine trees soaring straight into the sky. It was cold, and a little scary, but the adventure of it all outweighed the fear. The cabin door was frozen shut, and we had to pry it open. We turned on the heat, immediately lit a fire and gathered in front of it like a basket of kittens. I went to the sink to get water, but I was told I'd have to eat snow. The guys would go to the river in the morning and drill a hole through the ice and bring back a bucket of water for drinking. Okay then, snow it was.

One of my favorite feelings in the world is when my cheeks get hot in front of a crackling fire. I fell asleep on the floor. In the morning, we all stumbled outside to a glittering whipped cream world. We strapped on downhill skis and headed through the frosty trees, emerging onto a hill with skiers and a chair lift, so I guess the cabin was not as remote as I thought.

My strongest memory of the ski day was the last run. The fog had rolled in so you couldn't see in any direction. Everyone else had skied down, and I sat down in the snow. I dug my mitten into the powder and let it melt on my tongue while I thought about this moment.

It should have felt surreal, but I actually felt just right. Here I was, a girl from a little town in Utah, on the other side of the world, alone in the fog on a snowy mountain in Norway, listening to the quiet hush of falling snow.

I flopped onto my back and stuck out my tongue to catch a snowflake, moving my arms through the snow to make the wings of an angel. I felt giddy, like a carefree child, and I shouted, "Jeg Elska Deg!" And then clapped a mitten over my mouth. Who was I shouting to? The snowflakes? The mountains? The fog? There was nobody around but me.

I lay there for a while and thought about how memories are like snowflakes. Some melt before you can even see their shape, and some stick to your lashes and land lightly on your coat, so you can see their exquisite shapes before they dissolve. Then, thirty years later, if you're lucky, you can close your eyes and savor the delicate memory before it disappears.

A Magic Carpet Ride in Egypt

Something magical happened when I traveled in Egypt. I rode a camel named Moses around the ancient pyramids of Giza while the sky rumbled with thunder, finally cracking open with a rain so soft it felt like velvet cloak landing softly on my arms. My back straightened as I imagined I was an ancient queen, sitting on a golden throne on top of a camel.

The night before, I had dinner with an Egyptian family. As the intoxicating scents of cinnamon, cloves, mint, and ginger filled the air, the eight-year-old girl sitting next to me taught me how to say various phrases in Arabic. I had been a professional Middle Eastern dancer for many years, so I could speak Arabic in song lyrics. For example, I could say things like, "The night is melting" or "I'm am burning with the fire of jealousy…" Not particularly useful in everyday life, unless you are in a magical land where the air smells like turmeric and saffron, and the language sounds like poetry.

The house where I stayed was filled with laughing women, and when the men left to smoke their hookahs, the women turned on Arabic music and danced with raucous joy, their bare feet stomping on the marble floors and thick oriental rugs. I sunk my teeth into a fresh fig drizzled with honey, and watched their jubilant dancing.

That's when I felt the shift.

Something about being in the house with the grandmothers, mothers, and children, made me think of my own mother. My Mom was very different from me. She grew up with her Mexican family in San Diego, and her dream was to be a schoolteacher in a one-room schoolhouse. She ended up having six children, and went back to school to fulfill her dream when I was ten.

I was raised Mormon, and girls in my world were taught to sew and be quiet, with the singular goal of finding a husband. I hated sewing, I wasn't quiet, and I had no desire to get married. Like I said, we were very different.

But my Mom had another side, a magic side. Her sisters and mother were practicing witches. At our unusual family nights, my aunt read our tarot cards, while my other aunt read palms, and my grandmother told us family stories of treasure maps and hidden gold in the hills of Mexico. I liked this side of the family-- the wild stories ignited my imagination. That was the part of our family I liked best, and I would never fit into the mold of a pioneer mending socks while wearing a long gingham dress and a bonnet.

My Mom could never understand why I felt compelled to jump into adventures in faraway lands, and she would say, "Oh Marci, how do you do that? How do you dare to go to these places by yourself? Aren't you scared?" This perplexed me, because when I travel, I feel the opposite of scared. When I embark on an adventure into the unknown, I feel more at home than I do at home.

I don't know why, and it's difficult to explain. And when I don't know how to explain myself, it's best if I just dance.

The Egyptian women pulled me up from my chair where I was happily eating my figs, and motioned to me to start dancing. White chiffon drapes floated out from the open-air walls and I moved my hips to the lush Arabic songs peppered with the sound of the sea nearby. I felt my bare feet sink into a thick oriental carpet.

That's when the shift grew stronger.

The women shouted, whistled and clapped for me, and as I shimmied and swayed my hips, I suddenly thought of my mom. All the bad memories were suddenly gone, like a puff of strawberry smoke from a golden hookah. My mind was flooded with all the good memories: how she caressed my arm when I had a fever, turned me upside down when I was choking, and held me when I came home crying from school.

It felt like an awakening, there in the velvet air.

It was overpowering, and it changed me.

Maybe it was being in Alexandria, this ancient city on the sea, where Cleopatra ruled on her golden barge with purple silk sails scented with rose oil...

Maybe it was dancing with these women across the world where we didn't speak the same language, but we actually did, a language beyond words...

Maybe I was hypnotized by visiting the museums and seeing images of goddesses, mummies, crocodiles, golden thrones and crowns made of the sun...

Maybe it was watching a sumptuous belly dancer at a palace with peacocks and flamingos walking outside...

The next day, we left Alexandria, back to Cairo.

When driving in Egypt, I like to keep my eyes closed, so I don't have a heart attack. Cars speed and swerve, narrowly missing other cars, people, horses, and everything else. Our car finally paused, and I opened my eyes to see men on every corner, sitting outside wearing their galibeas and smoking the shisha. Across the street, the winding market stood, Khan el-Khalili. Glittering belly dance costumes, delicately shaped perfume bottles, spices, and tiny pyramids beckoned me, but I would visit them a different day. The car jerked forward again and I closed my eyes until we finally arrived at the pyramids. I climbed up on top of Moses, the camel. The way he walked made my body undulate, and I happen to excel at undulating. I channeled my inner queen, and Moses and I undulated together around the ancient pyramids, and I suddenly realized what caused the shift that reconnected me with my mother. It had to be the shimmering oriental carpet I danced on. Of course! I was in Egypt, an ancient land of peacocks, golden hookahs, and magic carpet rides.

Adventures with Kim
The 90's

Moonlit Balls, Seashell Crowns, and a Quest in Tulum

I had spent a rough month belly dancing in Mexico City. Kim came to rescue me and we traveled to the Yucatan to heal. The sea was so beautiful, so brilliant, we decided we should take some cheeky photos of us frolicking in the ocean wearing only our birthday suits for our Christmas cards back home. This quest for a Christmas photo led us on one divine adventure after another. The Yucatan is known for the Mayan fertility goddess Ixchel, and it was easy to feel like a goddess when you were spending your days rolling around in the warm turquoise waters with your best friend, wearing seaweed crowns and seashell bracelets.

One night, something rose over the sea, massive and blood red, turning the water red and pink. We weren't sure what we were seeing. We kept rubbing our eyes and wondering if it was something magical. When we realized it was the moon, Kim dropped to her knees and said, "I was going to wait until we got home, but this is too perfect. It's like our own kingdom here." She cupped her hands and handed me a shimmering moonstone she had bought for me that day on the beach.

I dropped to my knees next to her in the white powder sand and she tied the string around my neck and touched one finger to the stone. The moonstone on a simple string became a dazzling jewel when she took my hand and started to dance with me to the sound of the waves, finally laying her head on my shoulder as we watched the moon rise higher.

Kim passed away two years ago, but in my heart, we are still dancing on that beach. She is wearing a robe spun with shooting stars and I'm wearing a dress sewn from a sheet of rain. I can feel her hand in mine, and I wonder if somewhere, somehow, that sea still glimmers with the reflections of our moonlit ball.

Tulum

The Queen's Bath

I embrace new adventures, but belly dancing in Polanco in Mexico City for a month turned out to be full of the wrong kinds of adventures: people who didn't keep their word and a situation that was not even close to what was promised. Every night felt like I was dining with panthers, unpredictable and dangerous. That's when Kim, flew down and we hopped a bus for twelve hours to Palenque in the Chiapas Rainforest. We climbed and marveled at incredible ruins, the stones crumbling and covered in moss and made up stories about the people who had once lived there. We made our way over to a waterfall called The Queen's Bath. There were a few local families taking photos, and Kim and I stood off to the side to try to discreetly change into our swimsuits. Kim bent over in such a way that she was able to slip on her suit without anyone noticing. I followed her lead, and in my usual Inspector Clouseau bumbling way, I bent over facing the wrong direction and mooned everyone at the waterfall. Making matters worse, Kim screamed at my exposed behind, which made me jump, flashing even more people, as I flattened myself to the ground trying to wiggle into my suit as fast as possible, while Kim held up her shirt as a curtain and howled with laughter next to me.

We sat next to each other for a while, recovering, until everyone was gone but us, then we waded into the cold and gorgeous water, wrapping our arms around each other for warmth. We had been told the waterfall got its name because the ancient queens used to bathe here, but I thought of another reason: I have never felt more like a queen than swimming in a waterfall in a jungle surrounded by ancient stones with my twin soul, who put her arms around me when I was cold, dissolved tension with her deep laughter, and covered me when I was falling apart.

Waterfalls in Mexico

Laughing Myself to Sleep in Tulum

Kim and I met up with our friend Kayren in the Yucatan. We had all heard the stories about the dangers of traveling in Mexico for women. We were traveling on a local bus late one night, when it unexpectedly stopped at a rest stop. The energy seemed off, and several people appeared to be hanging around and "up to no good" as my father would say. I told Kim and Kayren to not make eye contact with anyone– just walk briskly in and out of the restroom.

Five minutes later, Kayren emerged from the bathroom singing loudly, with her sarong over her head, shimmying her shoulders, and spinning so her skirt flared out. All nervous tension dissolved as people started laughing and one stranger started dancing with her. They applauded for her when we boarded the bus.

We returned to our little hut on the beach in Tulum, $10 a night split three ways, and Kim and Kayren climbed into their hammocks to sleep. They had bought them a few days earlier with the intention of sleeping in them so we could save money. It didn't work out that way, and I knew they'd be cramming themselves into my little bed within the hour saying their backs hurt. Then, we'd all sleep piled on top of each other, so hot and sweaty in the morning, we didn't even say hello. We just opened the door and plowed into the glistening sea.

That night, I listened to the waves right outside our door, and it sounded like they were shimmying and dancing themselves, and for the first time in my life, I fell asleep laughing.

Fairy Hunting on the Isle of Skye

Kim and I went Fairy Hunting on the Isle of Skye in Scotland. Did we find a Fairy Kingdom full of singing, dancing, feasting, and wild delight? Did we explore crumbling castles and dance on Fairy Bridge and disappear into a magical world?

YES!

Kim and I had met each other when we were cast as fairies in a Midsummer Night's Dream in LA, so we were sure that if anyone would get to see a real fairy, it would be us. We were gallivanting around Edinburgh when we passed a little shop that matched ancestral names with tartans, and on a whim, I said, "Let's go find my family tartan!" I have a Scottish grandmother from the McClure Clan. We entered the shop and a small elderly man resembling a large mushroom, told me the McClure clan came from the Harris-McLeod clan, and our castle was on the Isle of Skye. Off to Skye we went. Back then, you had to take a ferry to Skye, and it felt like we were crossing to another world, a world of magic.

When we arrived on Skye, it was raining so hard we couldn't see the road. We found a room to rent at an inn, climbed a narrow curving stairway to our beds, and were thrilled when we found a bathtub, but not thrilled when Kim climbed into the hot water without noticing it was bright green. We asked the innkeeper what was happening and she said not to worry about green water, it was just the peat moss. I skipped the tub and opted for a hot shower instead.

The next morning, we put on our raincoats, and made our way to the castle, Dunvegan. We walked the hallways, imagining the centuries of ancestors who walked there, ran through the halls, fell in love, prepared for battle, and wept with loss after the battles… We stopped to look at a framed piece of torn dirty fabric on the wall, that had been mended several times with thick red thread. The plaque next to it read "Fairy Flag." A little old lady with hair like a dandelion puff floated up to us to tell us the story.

She told us that back in the 4th century, one of the chiefs of the clan fell in love and married a fairy. They even had a fairy baby, which explains so much about my love of dancing and glitter. She said the fairy had sewn the "Fairy Flag" with silk from the Middle East, and I imagined fairies wearing golden slippers with upturned toes gifting my fairy ancestor with the fine delicate silk, maybe folded on a velvet pillow. The fairy sewed the flag and imbued it with magic to protect the family. The clan carried the "Fairy Flag" into battle for centuries, which explained its dilapidated torn condition. The woman told us that even in World War II, the family carried a photo of the flag in their wallets as protection. We asked her if there were real fairies around the castle. Her eyes twinkled with delight as she nodded and said in her rolling accent, "Of course! The wee ones dance every night on the Fairy Bridge." (It sounded more like, "Of couddse, the wee ones dance everdddy night on the Feddddy Bdddidge.")

Kim and I walked out of the castle and deep into the surrounding wild woods, exploring every detail of the grassy hills where fairy kingdoms are known to exist, looking closely underneath vibrant polka-dotted mushrooms. We even stepped into mushroom rings, one at a time, holding hands in case one of us disappeared into Fairy World, a world known to be filled with music, dancing, feasting, and all sorts of pleasures and delights, which actually wasn't any different than our actual world. It is said that time runs differently in Fairy World.

If you step into a mushroom ring and end up in a Fairy Kingdom, you might be gone for twenty years, but it will only feel like a day.

I know exactly how Fairy Time runs because that's how it felt to be with Kim.

That night, we waited for the rain to stop so we could go to the Fairy Bridge and see some dancing fairies ourselves, but we both fell asleep, cozy under the puffy blankets at our inn. When we woke up, the air was shimmering with that light that only happens after a hard rain, when the raindrops on leaves, stones, and spider webs catch the light so it looks like the world is dripping in diamonds.

We went to the Fairy Bridge, but alas, we didn't see any dancing fairies, unless you count the two starry-eyed wanderers spotted leaping across the charming stones. If we couldn't find the magic, we made it ourselves. We passed crumbling castles and blue lochs. Kim excelled at making faces that resembled our idea of what a friendly loch monster might look like. We climbed stairways that ended in the sky, attached to nothing, and sat on the steps with our arms around each other, looking for any sign of magic.

Now that Kim is gone from this world, I like to imagine she's in a Fairy Kingdom somewhere, wearing a crown and carrying a long stick as a magic wand, maybe riding through a magical forest on the back of a purple dragonfly. I imagine she is singing, dancing, feasting, and bathing in one sun-splashed glittering raindrop. I like to pretend I am still holding her hand from this world, making sure she doesn't disappear.

"Come Away, O Human Child, To the Waters and the Wilds, With a faery, hand-in-hand, For the world's more full of weeping, than you can understand." (Yeats)

Chasing Rainbows on the Isle of Skye

There are songs and poems and endless legends about rainbows and I love them all. In fact, I consider myself a bit of a rainbow connoisseur. I have seen my fair share of rainbows, but nothing prepared me for the day we saw thirteen rainbows in one day on the Isle of Skye in Scotland. THIRTEEN! Kim and I were fairy hunting and researching my ancestry on the Isle of Skye. (Pre-internet, and if you wanted to research your ancestry, you had to go to the country where your family's stories took place and start asking around.)

After two days of rain, the sky changed into bursting rippling sunshine with rainbows appearing everywhere: full vibrant arched rainbows, half rainbows, double rainbows... Each time we saw one, we screamed and whipped the car around, driving to find the end, sure that we would find pots of gold.

We talked about what the pots would look like, would they be big or small? Would they be shaped like an urn or a soup pot? We passed dilapidated castles overlooking blue lochs, rolling green hills, and craggy rocks reaching up to a sky exploding in color. We were laughing so hard it was difficult to drive as the rainbow moved *yet again* and we turned the car *yet again*.

As the light of the sky changed, the rainbows changed, stunning us with shimmering colors shooting in all different directions. A massive vibrant glorious arch would appear and we'd cheer, and then it was gone, disappearing and reappearing in lush gorgeous colors. For one glorious precious moment, it was me, Kim, and the rainbows. Then they were gone from our sight, but here's a little secret: I can still feel the thrill of chasing the rainbows that day deep in my soul.

In the past, when people asked if we found any pots of gold that day, I said no, but now I answer yes. We found the pots of gold, but it was different than you think. The real pot of gold was in *looking* for the pot of gold: a grand adventure searching for magic with my best friend. Telling stories, laughing till we were doubled over, watching the lochs for signs of lake monsters, crawling through the woods hoping to see fairies... Even if Kim was still alive, our Day of Rainbows was a treasure more precious than any glittering pot. We didn't need to find anything except each other. That was the real magic. That was the biggest pot of gold.

Rosie's Hat Shop on Candlemaker Row

When I travel, I can't resist a quirky hat shop. While exploring Candlemaker Row in Edinburgh, I ended up in a hat shop called Rosie's. Kim and I, tried on hat after hat, taking on their personalities, from jaunty riding hats to French Riviera sunhats to Irish tweed newsboy caps. We decided new hats qualified as necessary purchases and we used Kim's emergency credit card for our purchases. (We paid it back later.) Kim was smart in her purchase, buying a Great Gatsby style hat knitted from soft cream chenille, perfect for traveling because it folded up smaller than a sock. I, on the other hand, did not choose wisely. I bought a large, stately, blue, structured hat, like Audrey Hepburn's hat in *Breakfast at Tiffany's*. It was impossible to pack, and since I was backpacking without my own personal bellhops, I had to wear it. My new hat fell low over my eyes, so I couldn't really see where I was going.

We swaggered into a coffee shop in our new hats. A cute boy (at least I think he was cute, I couldn't really see him) looked at Kim and said in a thick Scottish accent, "Ay, I see you've got a tea cozy on your head." Then he turned to me, "And what have we here? A lamp shade?" We all burst out laughing and ended up making plans for him to give us a ride to Inverness the next day, although he said my hat would have to be tied to the top of the car since it wouldn't fit.

Kim and I went back to our hostel and put on our velvet capes for dinner. (Did I mention we had already used our emergency card to buy "necessary" velvet capes in London?) While we stood on the corner of a cobblestone street discussing dinner options, several different sets of tourists walked up to us and asked if we were running ghost tours. We were tempted to answer yes, thinking we could make back the money we had spent on hats. We actually really wanted to go on the official ghost tours ourselves, but we were out of money. We hatched the brilliant plan of walking backwards towards the tour groups, hoping they wouldn't notice the two caped girls in hats lurking near that tree. They noticed, of course, and yelled at us that we weren't allowed to listen, at which point we ran down the steep hill barely lit by flickering lanterns, our capes billowing behind us like 18th century heroines racing into the dark night, but who needs a light when you can *be* a light by wearing a lampshade on your head?

Rosie's Hat Shop on Candlemaker's Row

A Hostel and a Towed Car in Belfast

We arrived late on a rainy night in Belfast and all the hostels were full. We lucked out when Arnie's Hostel had a cancellation and could give us two bottom bunks. Not ideal, as there were three of us backpacking at this point: Rogelio, Kim, and me. Rogelio was a friend I'd met one summer in South Carolina when I was visiting my twin cousins. We had become pen pals, then friends, and he was currently in the Air Force, stationed in England, so he joined us on this portion of our trip. So now in Belfast, we were desperate for a place to sleep. We said yes to three of us sleeping in two single beds. Kim and Ro took pity on me and said they'd share. We were directed to a room where two young men were laying on top bunks, reading. Kim and Ro settled onto the twin mattress in their pajamas with their heads at opposite ends.

We were all starting to settle into our strange surroundings when we heard a loud THWACK. The mattress above Kim and Ro somehow crashed through the bed frame, and the boy laying on it screamed as his knees were now touching his nose and his behind was stuck hanging down. Kim and Ro screamed too, but with laughter, just for a second before we calmed ourselves enough to help him out of his predicament. After we finally dislodged him, we fell apart laughing.

Earlier that day, we had visited the Giant's Causeway, some giant rock formations that happen to resemble giant boots. Now there are scientific explanations for the marvelous boot rocks, but I like to pretend giants roamed the land in ancient Ireland. Kim and I both loved stories that swept us away into an enchanting world of wonder and laughter, because they matched our best friend world, more than the everyday world.

The next day, we woke up from our rickety bunk beds and walked outside to find our rental car had gotten towed. NOOOOO!! This negativity didn't happen to us! We took a cab to the tow place and were horrified when we learned the price of getting it back. I tried to charm/beg the guy to give us back our car for a discount, as the price would use up all our traveling money. He shook his head with a firm no.

Kim and I sighed and stood on the sidewalk, thinking about what we should do now. The leaves crunched under our feet, and we started jumping around, trying to see who could make the loudest crunch. I was wearing my long colorful stocking cap in the brisk air, and Kim started chasing me, trying to grab my hat off my head while I ran screaming. I think we were a little punch drunk from that special lack of sleep that comes from sleeping in a hostel.

The tow guy was watching our leaf-crunching-hat-chase from his office, and after a while, he called us over and handed us our keys for free. I wonder what changed his mind? Did he suddenly feel sorry for two girls hopping around like crickets in the crunching leaves? ("Oh those two mentals are going to need all their cash.") Or did his Grinch heart melt at the sight of our joie de vivre in the face of such irritation? Or maybe he was some sort of secret genie who decided to add this moment to our list of magical things that happen while traveling. But the real magic was Kim. I called her my Merchant of Marvels, because whenever we were together, she made everything a marvel.

Ireland with Kim

Amsterdam: The Night Our Hotel Room Disappeared

When we arrived in Amsterdam in 1995, we saw a man standing in the train station holding a sign that said, "Apartment, $15 a night." It sounds strange, but back in the 90's in Europe, this was a common way to find a place to stay. Balthazar was a lovely gentleman who rented out a beautiful apartment to backpackers. It was a colorful place, with purple and orange walls. Our first night in the city, we looked for a place to perform to make travel money. We eventually wandered to the police station, and if I'm totally honest, we might have been a little giggly from the magic mushrooms we had snacked on at a local cafe. I couldn't find a word for belly dance in my travel dictionary, so I had to do charades with the police officers to describe what we were looking for. "Belly" (point to belly)… "Dance" (We'd dance around the police station.) It took longer than one would think for the officers to understand what we were asking, maybe because we couldn't stop laughing. And now that I think of it, can you imagine how entertaining it would be to be a police officer in Amsterdam? I would love to just spend a few days observing the kinds of people they have walking into the station.

In any case, back to our charades. I think what finally clicked for them was pretending I was playing finger cymbals over my head. They pointed and drew a path on our map with a red magic marker. The path led us to a Middle Eastern nightclub behind the palace calle El Turkije. Kim and I found our way there and auditioned on the spot for the managers and staff, even though I was wearing a turtleneck, skirt, and tights and Kim was wearing pink overalls and a big sweater. They hired us to perform our belly dancing acrobatic act for the next few nights. They also offered us a free place to stay above the restaurant, so we moved our things there.

The next night, we performed till midnight, and then headed out to explore the city by night. As performers, we knew most cities the best by night, as we slept most of the day. Amsterdam is charming and fascinating with priceless people-watching, especially in the middle of the night. We met many wonderful characters: Pinocchio! A lion whose mane looked exactly like my hair! Self-flushing toilets! (We had never seen a toilet like this before and we spent quite a bit of time walking in and out of the bathroom to make it flush on its own–just magic.) We landed at a cafe just before it closed at 3 am. We looked at the menu of offerings, and decided to try the strongest offering, something called "Super Silver Haze." True to its name, it truly does put you in a haze. We floated out of the cafe and I had the unpleasant sensation of my ears being on fire and no longer attached to my head. We discussed the condition of my ears and decided our best course of action was going to bed.

We walked back to El Turkije, turned into the alleyway where the entrance was, and it was gone.

Seriously, the entire restaurant had disappeared along with our things and our place to stay. We looked at each other, our eyes huge, then looked back at the wall that was now in place of the restaurant. I tapped my chin as we pondered what was happening. Did the entire restaurant just disappear? Were we in the right place? Or was this an illusion brought on by the Super Silver Haze? We walked up and down the alley staring at the wall.

And then things turned dark. Some guy eating French fries wandered down the alley way and nonchalantly asked us what we were doing. We said, "Our hotel has disappeared. It was right here."

He then said, "I wonder what you'd do if I decided to rape you." Seriously? In between your French fries you are going to attack us? Kim took off running in slow motion deeper into the alley. I grabbed her arm and said, "This way." My anger overrode my fear, and I marched past the French-fry-eating psycho, pushing him out of our way.

We looked for a policeman to report the scallywag. We saw a police car and two officers sitting in their car, eating French fries. Apparently this is what people did in Amsterdam at 4am — ate French fries. I told the officers about the guy and they listened, dipping their fries in a thick sauce. One officer said, "Did he attack you?"

"No, not physically. He just threatened us."

The officer shrugged. "What do you expect to happen to two girls in a dark alley in the middle of the night anyway?"

"You can't be serious! He threatened us! That has to count for sexual harassment at the very least. And we should be able to walk where we damn well please at any hour and not be threatened! Are scoundrels allowed to roam the streets because it's late?"

They shrugged and continued eating.

We were getting nowhere, so we decided to find a hotel. Thank goodness for Kim's emergency credit card! We found a beautiful hotel and checked in at 5am! We ordered toothbrushes to be sent to our rooms and took hot showers and fell asleep safely in crisp white sheets. It was lovely, a few glorious hours of luscious sleep. But as soon as we woke up, we checked out. We had more adventures to experience, and they weren't going to happen in crisp white sheets.

Postscript: We later learned that some restaurants and nightclubs pull giant metal walls down over their venue after they close. Who knew? The next day we were able to get back into the restaurant and retrieve our things. We decided we were ready to move on to our next adventure. Next on our trip? Paris!

A Spicy Night in Amsterdam

One night, Kim, and I were sitting at the Josephine Baker Bar in Amsterdam, when we decided we would find lovers. We were talking to some cute boys, and they told us to meet them later at a bar called The Watering Hole. So we were wandering the streets, dazzled and intoxicated by all the wonder that is Amsterdam, and every time we met adorable boys, we told them to meet us later at the Watering Hole. We walked and walked, and feeling a little weary, we finally sat down on a curb to look at the curved bridges and the canals swaying with glimmering lights, like we were sitting in a fairy tale town.

Suddenly, our fairy tale took a dark turn as a bicycle whizzed by us, nearly running over us. Surprised, we scooted closer together, as two more cyclists whizzed by with sharp comments in a language we didn't understand. We discussed how rude these riders were as it seemed they were almost TRYING to run over us. Finally, we stood up and realized we were sitting in a bike lane. We looked at each other, our eyes wide, and shouted apologies to the rude riders, but they were long gone.

We laughed all the way to the Watering Hole, where we were delighted to see our very own parade of darling boys. But when they saw each other, realizing they were all there to meet us, they all left!

This made us laugh even harder as once again we headed back to our rooms by ourselves. Our spicy adventures never seemed to quite work out, but we didn't care, we had each other, and that was the best spicy fairy tale of all. We put our arms around each other and skipped back to our room, careful to stay out of the bike lane.

Dancing on a Tabletop in Paris

I don't know why, but somehow, in my 20's, I ended up dancing on many tables. As a professional belly dancer, I have been pulled up to dance on hundreds of tabletops, but I'm surprised how often I have ended up dancing on tables while incognito, traveling in my regular clothes.

On our first night in Paris in 1995, we were exhausted from our long bus ride from London to Amsterdam to Paris, but we were in Paris, and we didn't want to miss a moment! Kim and I ended up in St. Michel, enchanted by the twinkling lights strung across the walkway, laughing with all the festive people, inhaling the smell of honey, baklava, and exotic spices wafting through the air. We were sauntering along, taking it all in, when I heard the familiar sound of live effervescent Greek music. I started to snap my fingers and swing my hips to make Kim laugh, and the owner shouted at me in French and waved me into the restaurant. There he pulled a chair in front of a table, and held out a hand to help me stand on it. I have no idea if it was actually a table or a tall barstool. I stood right up without thinking twice and started to dance. Whenever I end up dancing on a table or a barstool, the first thing I do is scan the people around to find the tallest person with the broadest shoulders, should the table collapse and I end up needing broad shoulders to keep me from landing on someone's grandmother.

This was the type of Greek restaurant that throws dishes and breaks them for fun, so as I danced, I watched the plates fly across the room smashing into the wall. The diners in the restaurant all stood up and cheered, forming a circle around me, whistling and holding hands and dancing together. Kim stood nearby, clapping and cheering, and every time I glanced over I could see her face beaming at me. One of the waiters linked arms with her and taught her some of the Greek dancing steps. I don't remember how long I was up there, or how I climbed down. All I know is that there are unforgettable moments when you are traveling, moments where you and groups of strangers who don't speak the same language, are suddenly swept into a moment so joyous, language isn't needed.

And now I had a moment to add to my collection of magical moments, where if people asked me what I did in Paris, I could say, "Oh, you know, the usual, I danced down the street under twinkling lights and ended up dancing on a table, surrounded by people so jubilant, I may as well have been floating.

Africa
1999

Missing My Plane to Africa

I missed my plane to Africa.

How did this happen, you ask? How in the world does someone miss their plane to Africa? Well… plane tickets used to be much harder to read, with a lot of cryptic numbers. You had to search to find the departure time, and there was always a good chance you were looking at the wrong numbers. I was happily biding my time, waiting to get there two hours in advance. I wandered the aisle of a store, looking at the different shampoos.

When I finally arrived at LAX, happily thinking I was two hours early, the airline told me the plane had left two hours earlier. I had read the wrong ticket—I had read the one from London to Nairobi, not LA to London. I shook my head in denial. This couldn't be true. The ticket agent shrugged. I begged her to just get me on the next plane going east. She found me a flight to NYC, where I begged the airline to get me on the next plane to London. I arrived at Heathrow at 9pm, and spent all my money racing to Gatwick, where I missed my plane by 30 minutes.

I ran inside Gatwick and it had shut down. I called the airline and they told me the next plane to Nairobi was the following night at 10pm. I had no way of reaching my safari to tell them I was coming. I also didn't have money to get back to London, so I spent my final $100 on a hotel room near the airport and tried not to spend money on food. Heading to Nairobi, I sat on the plane looking out the window. I had no idea what I would find when I arrived in Nairobi. Would my safari meet me? Would they be gone? Would I be on my own in Africa with no money? I had already paid for the safari, food, hotels, travel, so without them, I was… stuck. I decided I would think about it once I arrived.

As I slept on the plane, I opened my eyes for a minute and on the large screen, I saw myself! No I wasn't hallucinating. The plane was playing a recording of the Universal Studio premiere of a popular movie at that time, *The Mummy*, and I had danced on the red carpet at the premiere. It was a bit surreal seeing myself dancing with massive golden wings and jewels on my hips while on a plane to Africa, but I felt reassured that no matter what happened, I would figure things out. When I arrived the next morning, my safari was waiting for me. They had planned to spend the first night in Nairobi anyway, had called the airline, and knew I would be on that plane. My dance teacher and safari leader, Mesmera, said she had been so worried about me, but she had also seen me dancing with golden wings on the plane. She said, "Once I saw you spinning with your wings, I knew you'd be all right."

The Gift of the Masai Warrior

One afternoon in Amboseli in Africa, I was walking across a little bridge over a rushing river when I met a Masai Warrior with his long neck, shaved head, and beautiful smile. He was wearing a bright red cloak resembling a toga. He was adorned with colorful beads and seashells and carrying a tall a walking stick. He smiled at me. When I saw the magnificent colorful beaded band on his wrist, I gushed about its beauty. He didn't speak English, and I couldn't speak much Swahili, but it was apparent that I loved his wristband. He tapped it and told someone nearby that he had made it himself. The person translated his words to me. He took it off his wrist and gave it to me with a beaming smile. I put a hand over my heart, saying, "Thank you!" and put it on my wrist for the rest of my safari.

I hoped it was absorbing all the gorgeous eternal energy of Africa. I wanted to gift it to my best friend. Kim and I lived together in Hollywood, and she had been struggling with a deep depression that had led to her a suicide attempt. I had dropped out of school to care for her. Once she was stable, I had jumped on the safari to Africa to replenish myself. I couldn't imagine a better gift for her than a wrist band made by a Masai warrior, and I hoped it would protect her from the darkness.

Every night by the fire, I wrote letters home to Kim, telling her of the astounding animals I was seeing and the stars... my goddess the stars in Africa in that enormous sky... There is something about Africa that heals, something about the vast skies and storybook animals and the starlight. Under that huge sky, you feel small, but also big, part of a wondrous world where anything and everything is possible, and there are moments so beautiful, so magical, it makes the sad parts worth it. I wrote the letters in a small handmade journal I had bought so I could read them to her when I returned, which I did.

The main thing I wrote was this: *My love for you is boundless, timeless and eternal. Nothing will ever change that.*

I came across that journal and read her those words the day before her last and final suicide attempt last year. She said, "Thanks boo." in a small voice as the hot tears spilled down my cheeks.

When I went to her home and went through her things, finding our treasures together so I could bring them home with me, I opened a wooden jewelry box. Inside, was what looked like a dilapidated piece of trash with threads sticking out, but I recognized it immediately. It was the wristband. I pulled it out and clutched it to my heart. Oh my love, you kept it all these years. And now, I keep it in a Tiffany's box inside a drawer of precious treasures, along with my son's baby booties, and the fairy necklace Kim gave me. The warrior energy didn't end up protecting her, but I guess in the end, none of us could. I weep a lot over losing Kim, but I can tell you that the love remains, boundless, timeless, eternal.

It All Began with a Monkey and a Donut

Have you ever had a donut stolen out of your hand by a monkey? How about paperwork stolen by a baboon?

On my first morning in Kenya, I was walking through a breakfast buffet at my hotel, lit by candles because the electricity was only used at night. I stood in front of the donut tray, admiring the small monkey statue with its curled tail on the tray. I chose a powdered donut for my plate, and just as I was about to walk on, the statue sprung to life and whipped my donut off my plate. It grabbed a second one on its way out of the room, before catapulting itself up into a tree by its tail. It sat up high on the branch of a tree, nibbling my donut like it was a queen and I was its servant. I was a bit shocked, as there are no monkeys in Los Angeles. I stared up at it, admiring it's thieving abilities, and I swear it lifted one eyebrow at me as it nibbled.

A few days later, I was in Lake Nakuru in Kenya when I heard a ruckus. I saw a short person run by my window followed by a taller person, who was shouting. I ran to my door and saw the short person was actually a baboon. It stood about twenty feet in front of the shouting man with a bunch of papers in its mouth. It seemed thrilled by the chase, and I think it was actually waiting for the man to catch up a little so it could take off again at an uncatchable speed. Years later, I still think about that baboon, especially when I'm doing paperwork and wishing some baboon would come by and steal it for the best excuse ever. "I couldn't complete those forms, a baboon stole them." Sometimes I wonder if that monkey may have been a peddler of dreams. For the price of a donut, that monkey granted me a trip full of magic. I saw animals I had only ever read about in books, and animals I had never learned about, like bongos, zebroids, and pygmy hippos. What are these animals, you ask? Bongos look similar to deer, with thick red fur and wavy white stripes, like the frosting on a Hostess cupcake. Zebroids are a combination of a horse and a zebra, and pygmy hippos are miniature hippos. I didn't know there was such a thing, and while they weren't so miniature I could fit one in my teacup, they were close to the size of my footstool back home. They also weighed as much as a car. Just as enchanting was Speedy Gonzales, the hundred-year-old turtle, who moved like a dinosaur practicing tai chi.

For me, Kenya was the land of dreams, and it all began with a mischievous monkey and a donut.

Belly Dancing on Mt. Kilimanjaro

In collecting all my travel stories together, like gathering flying keys and putting them into an old wooden box, I have realized that my response to losing my greatest loves, best friends, soul mates, parents, husbands — is always to travel. Jumping into the unknown, going to a place where I've never been and I don't know the language, makes me feel lost, and somehow, helps me find myself again.

Dancing on Mt. Kilimanjaro was one of those moments where I felt lost and found at the same time. I went to the ancient mountain to dance back in 1999. That year was a year of transformation for me. I darkened my hair, went back to school, bought a reliable car for the first time and took up the cello. It had been a difficult, heart-breaking summer, rescuing the brightest light I had ever known, Kim. Once everything calmed down, I felt like I needed to heal my soul. My wisewoman belly dance teacher, Mesmera, had created a belly dance safari in Kenya. I decided to go two days before it started. Every day in Kenya was a mind-bending, soul-soaring adventure, from stopping our van for frolicking baboons in the dirt road, to watching a tower of ethereal giraffes float across our path, the sun setting behind their elegant silhouettes. We watched lionesses licking their paws in grassy fields while cubs tumbled around them, and we watched a leopard sleeping high in a tree, it's massive paws hanging off the branch like a teenager with one leg hanging off the bed.

One of my favorite moments in Kenya was a transcendent experience belly dancing with my silk rainbow veil on Mt. Kilimanjaro, while herds of elephants stampeded below us. Mesmera joined me on the cliff with her own veil, the warm wind whipping our veils. It felt like we were dancing in the sky. Back in LA, Kim and I had always called our home together the

Royal Palace, because whenever we were together, it felt like we were in our own kingdom. As I moved my veil through the Mt. Kilimanjaro sky, I felt like I was wrapping Kim in soft silk from across the world, surrounded by a sky so vast it felt like time and space didn't exist. Mesmera swirled her veil around next to me. When I finally fell to my knees on the rocky outcropping, weeping, she let me cry in peace and kept dancing. After several hours on the mountain, we drove back to our hotel during magic hour, right after sunset. A confusion of wildebeest and a dazzle of zebras surrounded the car, galloping around us in a frenzy. It was terrifying, beautiful, and exhilarating. As I stood up in the van with my head out the sunroof, it felt like we were part of the stampede, the van moving at the same pace as the galloping animals. That night I wrote to Kim. I told her how dancing on Mt. Kilimanjaro made me feel connected to something outside of time and space, something unbreakable and unchangeable, and that something was my love for her.

This bone-deep understanding is the gift Africa gave me. And now, I have a marvelous treasure safely stored in a rainbow silk scarf, some fragile fragments of a certain palace, a palace so beautiful you can still see its reflections in the sky over Mt. Kilimanjaro when the light is just right.

Incantation Bowl from Africa

Africa was magic for me. I bought a beautiful rosewood bowl somewhere along the way and I remember picking it up and inhaling the smell of the rosewood. I thought the bowl was so beautiful that I carried it around with me for twenty-one years.

My ex-husband hated it, and refused to let me use it in the house because he didn't like the smell of the rosewood. So now he's gone, and I get to use my treasured bowl. The kids and I had been using the bowl nightly for salads.

But now, the bowl has a new purpose, a perfect purpose, probably what it was meant for all along. After finishing the *Book of Longings* by spectacular author Sue Monk Kidd, I saw my rosewood bowl in a new light. The story centers on an "Incantation Bowl," a tradition in many ancient cultures. Women would choose a bowl and write their deepest heart's longing in a spiral inside, with an image in the center. They called it a "prayer to Sophia," the goddess of wisdom. It is said that if you run your fingers over it every night, your dreams come true. Run your fingers over it every night, I padded downstairs barefoot in my long nightgown. I pulled the bowl out and walked outside to lay it under the full moon.

I told the kids I was bathing the bowl in moonlight, and my daughter said," Oh great! Do you realize how crazy you sound? Bathing your bowl?"

(But then today, a few days later, she said, "Mom, do you know what manifesting is? I'm going to manifest my dreams.")

I could think of a hundred sentences for my bowl, but I couldn't pare them down to one beautiful sentence that would encapsulate my innermost secret dreams.

But the search for the sentence was paralyzing me, so I finally took a gold paint pen and just started writing random words that came to me, my own prayer to Sophia, in a spiral. I included the names of my beloveds, and I wrote down every word I could think of that I wanted to make sure was center stage in my life, words like love, light, laughter, moonlight, magic, generosity, abundance, kindness, open heart, open arms, open mind, writing, art, creativity, and Sat Chit Ananda, which means Being, Rapture, Bliss in Sanskrit.

I learned the Sat Chit Ananda words from reading Joseph Campbell. While at Harvard, I did a meditation ritual with my dear friend, Courtney, who wanted to make some changes in her life. Courtney was born and raised in Southern California and had never left. After the ritual, she packed up her car and moved to Alaska. She got a job at the local brewery, met her current husband, and now has two sons and is living out her dream.

So, maybe Sat Chit Ananda will work for me.

In any case, my bowl is gorgeous and I love it. The act of making it brought me such deep joy. With my love of sparkle, I did find it necessary to pour golden glitter into the bowl. I know in Japanese culture, they mend broken bowls with liquid gold, and the bowls are even more beautiful than when they weren't broken. They pour gold, I pour golden glitter. I'm hoping it will have the same effect as the broken bowls of Kitsungi. Maybe if I run my fingers over my wishes every night, my broken heart will heal and become more beautiful than it was before.

Paris
1998

The Red Phone

One of my favorite things about Paris is how they can make a train station look like a palace. Built in 1900, the Musee D'Orsay was originally built as an architectural wonder to welcome visitors to Paris. In fact, even though it was built as a train station, it was called the "Palace of Fine Arts." And oh how I wish all cities would create welcoming arrivals for their visitors. I live in Boston. When my visitors arrive at the airport and head north, they are driving through electrical plants, oil refineries, and eyesore after eyesore. I always tell my visitors to close their eyes until we get to the beautiful parts.

But for visitors arriving back in the early 1900's, Paris created magic.

So in 1998, my sister called me. She had found airline tickets for $180 round trip, so she, my other sister, and their husbands all bought tickets. I called my friend, Eric, a hilarious comic and actor, and asked if he wanted to go to Paris. He said, "YES!" and we were off. Our first museum? Musee D'Orsay. As we walked through the exhibits, my little sister burst into tears, missing her kids. I was busy marveling at the incredible marble Greek statues and their glorious renderings of the human body from ancient history. Turns out those ancient ones were in excellent shape, all with six packs and toned biceps.

I floated along the second story, gazing in wonder at the incredible building details, the light, the art. I saw a red phone on the wall all by itself, and I thought, "Oh cool, a little art installation. What delightful things might I hear?" I picked up the phone and put it to my ear, expecting to hear some wonderful story about art. Instead, someone started shouting on the other end in French. I thought, "My goodness this person is very passionate about art! Maybe it's some sort of performance art." Then several museum security guards and fully dressed firefighters came running towards me, shouting. I froze, unsure what was happening.

Was the museum on fire? Was there a burglary happening? Finally, Eric said loudly, almost shouting at me (okay, he was actually shouting) "Hang up the phone!" I hung it up fast, like it was a hot potato.

Ooops.

"I'm so sorry! Excuse moi!" I said over and over, adding a bow to show I was extra sorry.

The angry red-faced men threw their arms in the air in frustration.

I guess this is why my sister calls me Inspector Clouseau and follows me around when I'm baking cookies at her house, catching flying spatulas and dropped cookie sheets.

Eric and I quickly walked away, my face as red as the phone. He said quietly, "Why did you pick up the emergency phone?"

"I thought it was going to describe a painting."

He cleared his throat. "So, in all the museums we've been to, and all the art we've seen, we haven't seen one phone that describes a painting. But you thought...?"

Sigh.

"I don't know. It's Paris! The entire city is a living breathing work of art! It makes sense that a red phone in a museum would be art, or describe art, or at least recite poetry. And there is a kind of poetry in six sizzling firefighters running through priceless art towards me. Every time I think about fine art, that's what I think about.

A Magical Moment with Winged Victory

She is walking forward like she just won a mighty battle, her shoulders back, her robe rippling across her hips, her heart open, leading the way. This is no fearful wilting wallflower, oh no, this woman is exultant.

I was visiting the Louvre in 1998 with my dear friend, Eric, when I turned a corner and saw her standing in triumph at the top of the stairs. Chills ran up my arms, as I stopped in my tracks and stared.

Winged Victory is a 2,000-year-old marble sculpture of the goddess victory, Nike, which has been given a place of maximum impact at the Louvre, on top of an enormous stairway. Many people stood at the bottom of the stairs, and Eric and I joined them, gazing in awe.

I heard whispers next to me, and when I glanced over, I saw a young blind boy with an adult next to him, describing the piece of art. Without even thinking, hot tears spilled down my cheeks and a swirl of emotions made my heart feel like it was fluttering around my chest, trying to break free. What would it be like to walk through the greatest art ever created by humans and not be able to see it? What kinds of words was the adult using to describe this stunning 2,000-year-old sculpture? Was she able to paint a picture with her words, capture the wonder? The child looked like an ordinary boy, but as he listened to her whispers, his back grew taller and his shoulders rolled back, almost like his own invisible magnificent wings were spreading behind him. The woman linked arms with him and kept whispering while leading him up the stairway.

As my eyes traveled back and forth between the boy and Winged Victory, I felt my own invisible wings start to spread. This was twenty years before losing my father to cancer, my marriage to infidelity, and my best friend to suicide in the same year. I didn't know then how much I was going to need those invisible wings to get me through these staggering losses.

Experts speculate which ancient battle Winged Victory was created for, but does it matter? We are all fighting our own battles in our own way every single day. The fact that we are here, out in the world, celebrating the majesty of the human spirit through art, creating our own art, walking through these treasured creations, letting their astonishing beauty wash over us, is a winged victory in itself.

I wiped my tears off my cheeks with the back of my hand and walked on, with my shoulders rolled back and my dress rippling across my hips. Now twenty years later, if I happen across a photo of Winged Victory, I remember that boy. I lift my head higher, straighten my back to make room for my wings, and breathe steadiness into my shattered heart, reminding myself that I'm still here. And no matter how broken and bruised, my heart stays open and leads the way.

Drinking Red Wine Out of a Baby Bottle in Paris

Sometimes I feel like I'm the proprietor of a Curiosity Shop, but in my shop, the shelves are full of unique experiences.

Have you ever drank a tiny cappuccino in a little café in Greece as you watch the sunset over the sea?

How about a cup of warm milk with sugar served by a woman in a striped apron with a meat cleaver in her hand on a mountain in Switzerland?

Perhaps you've also eaten grilled squash served on a crumpled beer can in Basque country, cooked by a legend and his daughter?

Or drank a glass of crisp white wine in a dark cave in Norway?

How about drinking red wine out of a baby bottle in a crowded restaurant in Paris while eating fondue?

When I visited Paris in 1998, I read about a restaurant in Montparnasse called Chez Fondue that served its wine in baby bottles. BABY BOTTLES!

I was intrigued. Was it fantastic? Hilarious? Freudian? Disgusting?

I needed to find out. We climbed the steep hill to the intriguing restaurant with our entire party of eight people, consisting of my sisters, their husbands, Eric, and me.

The space was tiny and RAUCOUS, like someone opened a champagne bottle, put their thumb over the top and shook it. It smelled of bread, wine, and cheese. There were two long wooden tables with chairs jammed close together on each side. The empty seats were in the middle, so when the owner showed us to our seats, we all looked at each other. Who was going to crawl under or climb over the table? My sister, Maria, volunteered, even though she was wearing a mini skirt. She giggled as the owner helped her climb onto a chair and do a little leap to another chair across the way.

The restaurant only served fondue and red wine, nothing else. I don't even think they served water. And there were no glasses available, just baby bottles. My sisters are Mormon and don't drink, and I don't drink much, Eric, had six baby bottles full of wine set in front of him. They jammed as many people as possible into the restaurant, and our chairs were so close together, we had to hold our elbows to our sides while we ate our fondue, no easy task when you are eating with a long fondue stick. It was actually easier to feed the person across the table than to feed yourself.

So that's what we all did--we fed the person across from us.

The restaurant was so loud and riotous, it almost felt like it was going to cut ties and sail off into the sky.

I looked around at all the adults drinking red wine out of baby bottles and wasn't sure if it was entertaining or disturbing... a combination of both I think. Freud would have had a field day.

Eric was especially having a wonderful time with his six baby bottles full of wine. He became friends with the party next to us, even though it was impossible to hear what anyone was saying with everyone shouting over each other to be heard. It was one of those situations where you cup your hand to your ear to try to hear, and study lips to try to make out the words. Eric is a hilarious comedian, and even without talking he can make everyone around him laugh with his facial expressions. We fed each other fondue from across the table, in between all the laughter and yelling, and I sat so close to my sister I may as well have been on her lap. The wine was flowing, the cheese was bubbling, and as the owner walked by, I held my baby bottle up to him in a toast: bravo to the people creating unforgettable experiences and cheers to the adventurous ones seeking them out.

Italy
2000

The Legend of Elba

Long ago, I was standing in a café in Florence, dipping a warm chocolate croissant into my foamy cappuccino, when I heard the legend of Elba. A young woman wearing soft pink tulle and ballet slippers told me the story, her long red hair falling over her bare shoulders, as she talked in a voice so warm and buttery, I wanted to dip it in my cappuccino along with my croissant. Her hair made her look like a mermaid who was spending the day on land. She said that seven jewels, or pearls, fell off the necklace of Aphrodite, Goddess of Love, and landed in the sea off of Tuscany, becoming the Tuscan archipelago. The centerpiece of the necklace, the most beautiful jewel of them all, became Elba.

I was spending my summer of 2000 in Florence, studying Italian and Italian Cinema. With visions of mermaids and glittering jewels dancing in my head, I bought a ticket and hopped a ferry to Elba.

The only fact I had ever heard about Elba was about Napolean's exile there. I mean, can you imagine hearing you're being exiled and must live in paradise forever? That's a punishment I'd happily take any day.

I arrived on Elba at night, the smell of pine trees, rosemary, and lavender filling the air. The sky over the island was filled with so many stars I could clearly see in the dark. I dragged my backpack around from place to place, trying to find somewhere to lay my weary head. The place where I landed overlooked the sea, and in the morning, I lay on my pillow and watched the sunlight dancing on the cobalt sea like thousands of sparkling diamonds.

I headed out to a remote beach, nestling my towel in between some large cliffs. The warm sand cushioned my elbows as I lay on my stomach, reading a book. I was just wishing a pina colada would somehow float to me, when a small "Cocktail Boat" pulled up to shore, selling snacks and drinks. What kind of island was this, where I had only to think "I wish for a cocktail" and one appeared? I gleefully waded out into the waist-deep water, and bought some drinks and snacks to last me the afternoon. With a cheery wave from the driver, the boat sped away.

The water was so gorgeous and foamy, like I was wading into my morning cappuccino, so I laid everything down on my towel and walked back out into the water. I plunged my entire body under water, kicking my legs together like I would if I was a mermaid and the water caressing my body was thousands of tiny flaming sapphires. With my head under the water, I felt small and enormous at the same time, like a tiny delicate wave *and* a massive thundering ocean. I felt completely alone, but also deeply connected to everyone I have ever loved. It was the open sea: danger and darkness lurked, but so did the most beautiful vibrant light imaginable. I popped my head out of the water and breathed in salt and sunshine before flipping onto my back and floating, my eyes closed.

It was the year 2000, and though I had experienced my share of sadness, I did not know then how much heart-shattering loss was waiting for me in the future. I look back at thirty-year-old Marci, and I want to hug her, prepare her somehow for the massive pain that awaits, but there is no preparation for what is headed my way.

Or maybe there was. Maybe the "preparation" was meeting a mermaid in a café who told me stories that sent me on an adventure. Perhaps the secret to healing broken hearts lies in looking up at glittering stars in a dark sky, swimming in a glorious sea that can turn from dark and stormy to brilliant and clear in an instant, listening to fairy tales and legends, and the deep understanding that the most precious jewels in my life are the experiences, the times I said yes: yes I'll take that trip, learn that language, dance in that fountain, take a moment to watch the girl with the long red hair dance in the Piazza... If I was a Love Goddess, my precious necklace would be made up of a string of magical moments, experiences that I will treasure forever, that can never be taken, lost or stolen, or dropped in the sea.

Or maybe magical moments should be dropped in the sea, and every time we plunge ourselves in to swim, we are swimming in all the dazzling magical moments of others who have also plunged into the swirling sea. And maybe that's why it feels so wondrous and healing to swim in Elba.

Some people have coins and jewels in their Treasure Chest, I keep mine full of stories...

Being Robbed in Italy

Of course I don't enjoy being robbed, but as an adventuress, I have been robbed a few times; from waking up to some scalliwag trying to take my backpack out from under my head, to standing on a crowded bus and noticing some joker unzipping the zipper of my backpack. Sometimes they succeeded, sometimes they didn't, darn scalliwags and jokers.

So in the year 2000, I headed to a Study Abroad in Italy through UCLA. After spending a few days exploring Lake Como on my own, eating lunch in charming outdoor cafes and watching the moon shimmer on the lake at night, I lugged my suitcases to Florence. When I got off the train, I realized my small backpack was missing. Of course it was the bag where I kept my most important items: my passport, my return plane ticket, (pre-internet, you had to have the physical ticket), and my favorite red bikini.

My heart sank like a boulder in a crystal lake, and I ran to the Carabinieri, the Italian police inside the train station. I tried to explain the theft through a combination of pantomime, charades, and saying, "Mi pasaporte, poof!" with a hand clap, over and over again. The handsome young officer nodded solemnly at my story. I was relieved when he held up one finger, pulled out an official looking paper, and went to another officer, to have something filled out in English. He proudly handed me the paper, and it said, "Will you go to the fireworks with me tonight?" His expression was so hopeful that I burst out laughing. I shook my head and all the other police started slapping him on the back and speaking loudly in Italian. It was clear that no one was going to be looking for my backpack, and while going to see fireworks with this cutie sounded dreamy, I needed to get to my school.

When I told my professor about the stolen passport, she said, "You don't seem very upset about it." I shrugged. Passports can be replaced, I was more upset about my red bikini, which would be harder to replace. (I don't know why people get all stressed out about passports. I thought my ex-husband was going to blow a gasket when I accidentally threw out all our passports after returning from a trip to Anguilla. In my defense, they were all in a crumpled dirty envelope that looked like trash.)

So years later, I was reading a book to my kids about a wise panda bear named Stillwater. In the book, a raccoon bandit comes in to rob the bear. Instead of clobbering him, Stillwater says, "Are you cold? Here, take my robe." He hands the bandit his robe, his only possession, and then he goes and sits happily under the moonlight, saying something like, "Who needs things when we've got the moon?" After being robbed so many times, I have come to feel the same way.

Who needs things when I've got the moon?

Treasure Chest
Full of
Random Stories

I Played a Backpacker Before I Became One!

I actually played a backpacker in a commercial before I became one. I was living in Utah with my parents, trying to save some money before heading back out into the world, when I was cast in a British Airways commercial. I was a "rucksack girl", meaning I carried a backpack. We were transported to Moab, the red rock desert in southern Utah, where we all stayed in a one-level motel with doors that opened directly into a parking lot. We all went to a local bar that night, even though we had to be on location at 5am. It was a rough 4am wake-up call, and if you know the desert, you know it can be freezing at night, no matter how hot it gets during the day. I was sent into hair, makeup, and wardrobe. I was given an outfit I didn't love: blue denim Bermuda shorts and a blue top. They gave me a backpack to carry and stuffed a few shirts into it to give it some weight and a "realistic look". We filmed out on a steep and vibrant red cliff all day. My filming time lasted about ten minutes.

For the rest of the day, I laid on the smooth warm red rock, ate snacks from the snack table, and watched filming. The commercial aired during the Superbowl in 1988, and back then there was no replay. You watched the TV till your commercial came on. I screamed when I saw myself flash onscreen for one second, looking over my shoulder while climbing a cliff. Maybe that's what inspired me to become a backpacker, because at the time, I had never met one. Whether it did or not, one year later, I packed up my things into one big backpack, bought a Eurail pass for $250 so I could hop on and off the trains, and had an adventure, a million adventures, that changed me in ways I could never have imagined.

Border Patrol Meets Girls Marked Danger

It probably wasn't the best idea to practice my Spanish on a Border Patrol officer, but it was the middle of the night and I was giddy from performing, so I wasn't thinking clearly.

I was dancing on tour with The Go-Go's in 1999 with two dear friends and fellow go-go-dancers, Pleasant and Kina. It was 2 am, and we were road tripping back to LA from our show at the San Diego Bowl. We were discussing possible names for our go-go dancing group, finally deciding we should call ourselves, "Girls Marked Danger" after a Sophia Loren movie, although there was nothing dangerous about our job, unless you call sneaking out onstage like ninjas and climbing onto go-go boxes to dance, dangerous. We would climb onto the giant go-go boxes built just for us, wearing our sequin hot pants and go-go boots, and dance our cheeky choreographies until the curtain dropped. It was late, and I was giddy from performing for thousands of people on a hot summer night when I pulled up at the required stop at Border Patrol. I have no idea why there was a Border Patrol stop when leaving San Diego, but every single car had to stop. I must have been a little punchy, because I rolled down my window, and cheerfully said the three sentences I know really well in Spanish: Hola! Como Estas? Hablo Espanol un poquito."

The Patrolman wasn't amused. He pointed to my car and the curb, ordering us to pull over. I said, "I'm just kidding. I don't even speak Spanish."

He pointed again and added an even more gruff, "Pull over."

"Cello! What are you *doing*? Why are you speaking Spanish?" Pleasant asked, zipping up her jeans. She had eaten too much in our dressing room and was riding with her pants unzipped. Also, she called me Cello because I had recently started taking cello lessons. Up till then she had called me Marchella, but that was now shortened to Cello.

I answered, "I was practicing my Spanish! I didn't know they'd pull me over for it."

Kina was also perturbed. I was unaware that someone had given her two joints, which she had stuffed into her pocket, so when the officers made us get out of the car and sit on the curb, she acted very nervous. She kept saying, "I have to use the restroom," so she could get rid of the joints, but I kept saying, "Don't use those port-a-potties!! They are gross! I'll take you to a clean bathroom."

You can imagine how happy she was with my discouragement.

When the officers brought out their German Shepherds to sniff around my car, pushing aside my cello to do a thorough search, we all held our breath. Belinda, the Go-Go's lead singer, had put a big bottle of tequila in the back of my car as a gift, and it had spilled. "Why does it smell like alcohol?" The officer asked. "Hairspray!" I said, thinking quickly. I had heard somewhere that tequila and hairspray smell similar, or maybe it was vodka and hairspray. I don't know? The guards didn't find anything in my car. Before we climbed back in the car, we asked the officer if we could take a photo for our collection of cop photos. We had cops come to our parties with some frequency to tell us to quiet down. Sometimes we ended up taking photos with them, around their car, and on an especially festive night, they turned their flashing lights on for us.

I did learn a valuable lesson from this experience: next time I pass a Border Patrol, or any sort of international customs stop, I will take advice from The Go-Go's and keep my lips sealed.

The Dating Game

Fun fact: My love of traveling combined with my lack of travel funds has led me to some very interesting places. First stop? The Dating Game in 1988 where I won a trip to Hawaii! I was living in Hollywood, when I saw an ad for The Dating Game. I went to the address and two days later, I was on the set filming! It was a bit of a whirlwind.

I was the "Chooser," meaning I would be picking one of three bachelors behind a wall. I wore a black wrap Betsey Johnson dress I found on sale for $20, and of course I was having one of those "bad hair days" where no amount of hairspray or brushing will make it look presentable. I don't remember a word of their answers because I was too nervous with the lights, cameras, and studio audience. I do remember asking the following question: "My favorite meal is chocolate chip pancakes with toasted marshmallows for dessert. What's your dream meal?"

I tasted chocolate chip pancakes for the first time when I was 16, while traveling, and I never looked back. I still don't remember my bachelor's answers, but I vividly remember jumping up and down when I opened the envelope with our "prize" and it said, "Waikiki Beach Hawaii!"

I traveled with a perm, one suitcase, golden mummy earrings and a teddy bear named Binky. No, I didn't love my date. He was nice, but wanted to eat at McDonalds and stay by the pool while I wanted to be out exploring all day. Everywhere we went, people somehow found out we were from The Dating Game and asked to take our pictures. I was transfixed by my first luau even though I may have spent more time looking at the empty bottom of my pina colada pineapple than watching the show. I tried to enjoy snorkeling around Hanauma Bay but the stealthy fish kept startling me, giving me a mouth full of salt water.

On our last night, we took a sunset catamaran sail and ended up hanging over the side vomiting, wishing I could swim back to shore. I dove off the catamaran and let the warm seawater wash away my seasickness. I wanted to swim for a while, but we were so far out I couldn't see the shore, and I tried not to imagine what sharp-toothed creatures might be lurking beneath me. When I climbed back onto the catamaran, I wrapped myself up in a fluffy towel, and as the pink light of the warm sky wrapped and fluttered around me like a grass skirt, I thought I had never seen a sky so beautiful. I knew it would disappear within a moment, so I watched it change colors off the back of the catamaran as we caught the wind and sped back to shore.

Traveling Wardrobe

I don't know why planning my travel wardrobe is one of my favorite parts of traveling, but it is. Maybe it's because I adore the Golden Age of Travel where people had matching luggage and gorgeous travel outfits. Maybe it's because I like to pretend I'm living in an old Technicolor musical and wearing colorful dresses helps me create my own universe. Or maybe it's just because I love the way clothing tells a story about the person wearing it.

For example, when I go to Texas to visit my sister, I wear cactus dresses and sparkling crystal cowgirl boots.

Kim, used to shake her head at me and say, "You sure love to dress in themes!" She said this when I was wearing a cherry red 1950's sundress I bought at a thrift shop for $5, with a ponytail in my hair, a red scarf tied in it, matching sunglasses and bright red lipstick. She was right, I dress in themes.

When I visit California, I wear my baby blue avocado dress. When I go to Salem, MA, I wear a dress covered in black cats, and when I went to Venice last summer, I wore a dress with images of the city and gondolas printed around the bottom of the skirt. If I want to feel festive, I wear my bright green dress with hot pink dancing girls and circus acrobats across the skirt, and if I want to be a bit more subdued, I wear my sage green and deep purple New Orleans dress, with horses and carriages and lanterns trotting around the bottom of the skirt. I may be the only person on the planet who views this dress as "subdued," but there you have it.

Maybe it all started when I took my first plane ride at the age of twelve. We were flying from California to Chicago, and my Mom bought me my dream outfit for the plane ride. What was my dream outfit in 1981? A white turtleneck with hot pink reindeer leaping across the chest, hot pink "knickers" which were pants that pulled in just below the knee, and a thin gold belt. Alas, I had the flu when we flew, so I couldn't really enjoy my favorite ensemble. I have one photo from that day, and I could barely lift my head, the leaping reindeer a slap in my ghost-white nauseous face.

Before heading out on my safari to Africa, I watched *The African Queen* with Katharine Hepburn and Humphrey Bogart to get in the mood, along with old clips of Rita Hayworth when she was dating Prince Aly Khan. I went and invested in a wardrobe of 1940's style khaki suits, complete with pencil skirts and fitted blazers with pockets. But when I came home and laid out my wardrobe to show Kim, she shook her head and said absolutely not. She said I must return it all—too hot, too itchy, too uncomfortable for 5am jeep rides to see cheetahs and giraffes.

Sigh. She was right. I returned it all for more comfortable safari clothes, like silk tiered skirts and tank tops. While planning my wardrobe, I happened to visit my seamstress, a little person named Alexis Caramelo who lived in Hollywood with his Chihuahua named BooBoo. Alexis had an earth-toned polka dotted umbrella sitting on his crafting table, the edges lined in orange pom-pom fringe. It seemed perfect for Africa, so I bought it from him without even thinking of the fact I would now need to increase my suitcase size to fit the umbrella. I wasn't sure how much I would use it on my safari, but I ended up using it every day. I took it out in the canoes to shade me and carried it when we toured ancient Arabic ruins. I used it almost as much as my silk rainbow veil, which I danced with several times a day.

And then... I entered the dream of all vintage travel style

lovers... the Grand Poobah of wardrobe dreams--the Orient Express. This glamorous train requires dressing to the nines, and I enthusiastically embraced the challenge. This was my chance to indulge my most elaborate vintage style fantasies: retro dresses with fluffy petticoats underneath, hats with jaunty plumes, wrist gloves for daytime, colorful heels and matching purses, elbow-length gloves and long gowns for evening. And for our gentleman, my 13-year-old son, bow ties, blazers, boots straight out of the 1800's and bowler hats. Planning our wardrobe was nearly as much fun as the actual trip!

I made life easy for myself on our entire trip to Europe by packing twenty retro style sundresses, seven tutus, a few big floppy sunhats, and two sparkling evening dresses that also didn't wrinkle. We packed our main suitcases, and then our Orient Express bag, which was full of our floor-length silk evening gowns, pearls and tiaras, velvet jackets and elbow length gloves. And of course we had our hatboxes. I wasn't going on this amazing train without my hats. They have jaunty curling feathers, which required special handling so they didn't crush. That meant vintage hatboxes that had to be carried separately from our luggage. "My goodness!" You may be thinking. "How many suitcases did you take?" My answer? A lot. But I long for the era of traveling with multiple steamer trunks, where I could fit anything and everything in my suitcases, from my belly dancing costumes to my ice skates, roller skates, day wear and evening wear.

And, of course, we must not forget the handbags. I love a cheeky handbag. When I bring my sparkling champagne bucket purse, it's like traveling with Beyonce. People ask to take photos with it. I have a red wicker baguette bag, perfect with my cherry dress, and I have a bag that looks just like a basket of strawberries, which I wear with my strawberry dress. I just bought a Jetsons space dress to match the rocket handbag I fell in love with a few years ago, but didn't have anything to wear it with. See what I mean? Themes.

I do bring my novelty bags because… obviously… they delight me. Overall, however, I don't like carrying short handbags while traveling. I like to have my hands free because I'm usually walking all day long. This requires an over-the-shoulder bag, and I found the perfect one. It was made of soft white faux fur with floppy ears and whiskers… yes it was a bunny. Kitschy and fun, it could fit my phone, lipstick and wallet, and was so soft it was like carrying a stuffed animal. And shockingly, it stays white even though it has traveled all over the world with me.

Over the years, my unique sartorial travel style has evolved into me dressing more and more like I am starring in my very own 1950's MGM musical. For some reason, beautiful clothing makes it easier to cope with the world, a colorful tutu under my dress makes me feel like twirling, and feathers soften the edges, making the world seem gentle and romantic. So when you travel with me, just plan on my pink suitcase popping open in a spray of colorful tutus and glittering treasures. It's all part of the magnificent journey.

More Healing Trips
2018-2019

Venice: Extravagant Costumes, An Opera in an Ancient Palazzo, and Dancing Barefoot Under the Moonlight

On my half-century birthday, and I decided it was time to check some things off my bucket list. Traveling with my teenagers was top on that list.

First stop… Venice!

I love Venice. and on this trip, I had a bucket list destination: the Atelier of Antonia Sautter, a spectacular historical costume creator. Antonia creates incredibly extravagant events every year, including a ball, Il Ballo Del Doge, that is listed on Vanity Fair's Bucket List as well as my own. I love costumes, and I love parties, so of course Antonia Sautter would catch my eye.

We arrived in Venice, dropped our luggage at our hotel, and went straight to Antonia's studio. When I say straight, I mean we walked down winding cobblestone alleyways until we found the address, which turned out to be very close to our hotel. There was no door, so we knocked until someone poked their head out from an upstairs window and directed us down more curving cobblestone alleys to another secret door. We climbed the steps towards a stunning feathered headdress, and my heart started the little dance it does when I see feathers. The studio felt like being dunked in someone's incredible fantasy world.

Massive ballgowns, easily six feet wide, long trains, jewels winking from every piece of fabric, tiers of frothy lace, huge headdresses with feathers, sumptuous brocades, shimmering silks, tiaras and crowns and capes... The opulent handmade textiles, the silk velvets stamped in gold or with bejewels dragonflies lit me up brighter than fireworks over the canals.

Antonia creates many historical gowns based on the actual gowns of such decadent dressers as Marie Antoinette and Madame De Pompadour. They even let us try on some of the headdresses. While the studio offers different tours, we chose the historical one. You can pay a little more and try on gowns. For a lot more and you can go outside and run around the streets of Venice, into a gondola with a photographer in tow. This sounded dreamy to me, but I had scrimped and saved to take this trip and gallivanting around Venice in gorgeous costumes wasn't going to be on our list this time. The tour of the studio *was* on our list, and it was a fantastic introduction to a divinely decadent city.

Our first evening, we ate at the charming Da Ivo. We dressed in our fancy clothes and made our way through the winding cobblestone alleyways to an adorable little restaurant nestled on the water. Cozy and oozing with charm, with seasonal food that exploded with flavor, Da Ivo was the perfect Venetian restaurant. We all agreed it was the best spaghetti we had ever eaten.

The next day we walked across the historic Pontevecchio bridge to the Guggenheim. I love everything about the Guggenheim, especially it's history. Over the years, it was owned by three different heiresses: Doris Castlerosse, Marchati Luisa Casati, and Peggy Guggenheim. All three were known for supporting artists, creating elaborate parties and parading through Venice. Peggy Guggenheim was a fabulous supporter of artists. She left her house and art collection as a museum. The art is whimsical and fantastic. I was delighted to hear my niece, Zoe, ask one of the guides about the difference between Dadaism and Surrealism. I'm never very clear on the difference myself. The young woman told Zoe that Dadaists used their art to try to destroy reality to nothing, while the Surrealists take reality and bend it into something fantastic, beyond reality.

Our trip was a combination of both living Dadaism, as we destroyed our painful reality from back home with fresh new experiences, and Surrealism, as we bent that pain into beauty, art, and magic on our journey.

On the path of healing, I was embracing all of the things I deeply loved but had lost during my marriage. One of those things was opera, which I had fallen in love with as a sixteen-year-old girl in Utah. My school took us to the ornate Capitol Theater in Salt Lake City, and I was completely transported. I didn't know theaters could be so beautiful. I couldn't think of a better way to introduce my kids to opera than attending one in an ancient Palazzo on the water. The opera company was called "Musica Palazzo," the "theater" was the Palazzo Barbarigo Minotto on the Grand Canal, and the opera was the *Barber of Seville*. Again, we dressed in our fancy clothes and walked through winding streets to find the palazzo, finally turning a corner into a dark alleyway where Zoe whispered to me to hang onto my purse. The alley led us to the gorgeous crumbling palazzo, the steps lit by candles so you felt like you were stepping back in time.

The Palazzo Barbarigo Minotto is located on the Grand Canal and was built as a 15th century gothic palace. The Barbarigo family were an aristocratic family. Their name came from a family member who defeated pirates in the year 880 and returned with six of their beards. Their coat of arms has six beards on it! This story amazed me as I wondered what it might have been like to carry six beards around. How did he carry them? Were they whole? Still on chins? Or just the whiskers? Ooooh yuck.

We were seated on chairs in a massive living room and when the singing began, those lush voices echoing around those ancient walls, I got chills and tears pooled in my eyes. The singing transported me, like a flying ship full of all my lost loved ones, holding out their hands as they sailed overhead, pulling me onto the ship and whisking me away on a fantastic journey before plunking me back into my chair in this fairy tale city with my beautiful children and niece next to me. I landed back into the exquisite beauty of a very simple feeling -- a feeling of coming home after a long journey.

After those lush scenes concluded, the entire audience moved to the parlor, where more scenes were sung, including a hilarious song about a dog. The singer entered the room carrying the "dog," which was actually a wig on a leash. From there, we walked into a beautiful antique bedroom for the final scene. I kept closing my eyes, just savoring the moments, listening to the soaring voices with my beloveds next to me in a palace on the water.

After the opera, we were walking back to our hotel, when we decided to go to the Piazza San Marco for gelato instead. It turned out to be the best night of our entire trip. Walking in Venice at night with the twinkle lights reflecting on the water, the storybook bridges, and the ancient palazzos was a dream. The Piazza was nearly empty and freshly scrubbed. The outdoor cafes were still open, two bands were playing, and music filled the night air. The kids ended up dancing barefoot around the square under the moonlight. They had most of the Piazza to themselves, so they could twirl and leap and sashay as much as they wanted. In true travel style, different people stopped to talk to us, including some drunk British students with a wet soccer ball they had just fished out of the canal. My niece happens to excel at soccer. When they kicked the ball to her and saw her skills, they started To cheer.

I ate my gelato as I looked at the cobblestones beneath my feet, and wondered how many people had danced on this very spot. The first chapel was built on this site in the year 819. 819! I savored my Stracciatella and thought about all the people who lived and loved and left here so long ago. I wondered what they would have thought if someone had told them that eleven centuries later, the Square would still be filled with people from all over the world, students starting out their lives; elders living on memories; musicians weaving a magical spell; and broken-hearted mothers trying to protect their growing children...

I sighed as I watched my children dance. I wished I could give them back all that we had lost: their grandfather, their original family, their auntie... but I could not. What I *could* give them, was this magical moment, this one sumptous summer night in this fairy tale city, a moment I hope will give them a sweet place to visit when the world turns bitter.

***In an amazing example of synchronicity, I posted a story about this incredible night in the Piazza on Girls Love Travel, and a woman messaged me saying, "On my first night visiting Venice, I went to the Piazza and saw a girl dancing in a red dress. I took a video of it. I think it was you." She sent me the video and it was, indeed, my daughter dancing in a red dress, my son and niece, twirling around her, and I am standing there in my black tulle dress covered in silver glitter stars, watching over them. I cried when I read her message.

Standing at the Doge's Palace in Venice

Magic On the Orient Express

Right now, tonight, on this moonlit night, I am dreaming of trains, and specifically the luxury train to end all trains: the Orient Express. Last summer I took my teenagers on an unforgettable epic journey, a trip to a magical world we had only read about in books.

When I was a child living in Utah, I used to love hearing the Southern Pacific railroad blow its whistle in the distance. It made me happy to know someone was going somewhere, and I liked to imagine who they were, what they looked like, and where they might be going. I couldn't wait until I was old enough to go on life's adventures too. When we went anywhere, all six of us kids piled into our orange VW bus, sitting on the blankets my father had placed on top of our suitcases in the back.

When I entered the wild terrain of my teen years, I would come home from parties and before entering my house, I would sit down on the steps of my porch and listen to the train whistle. I loved the quiet of 2am on warm summer nights. I leaned my head against the wooden porch beams, listened to the crickets and the train, while smelling freshly mowed grass and the wet soil of the petunias my father lovingly tended every day.

Flash forward…

In 2018, my 50th birthday was on the horizon, and Kim and I had been planning to do something epic for my half-century birthday. We spent many hours talking about our ultimate travel fantasies, but life had a different plan in store for us. Kim didn't make it to my 50th birthday, and losing her turned my world upside down. The kids and I were devastated by her death. I didn't know what to do or how to make it through the thick swamp of grief for all of us, but I knew how travel was always healing to me. So on my birthday, I created a treasure hunt for my kids and at the end, they found tickets (handmade by me) along with the book, *Murder on the Orient Express.* They screamed, jumped up and down and threw their arms around each other and me. As the mother of teenagers, I don't get these moments often anymore. I like to consider myself a matador, able to handle their wild charging emotions with the swirl of a scarf and the tip of my hat. At least that's how it is in my mind. Planning an epic trip gave us months of swirling scarves, as we spent many mealtimes talking about what wondrous things we would experience together.

Now I could deeply indulge my love for the Golden Age of Travel style with steamer trunks and vintage hatboxes. You can imagine that for a mystery writer who loves glamorous travel style, the first place they are going to head is straight to the Orient Express. Made famous in Agatha Christie's brilliant mystery, *Murder on the Orient Express,* the train is legendary for its inspirational style, attracting artists, movie stars, filmmakers, and writers for more than a century. The storied train started rolling back in 1883, and passengers over the years might see Tolstoy, Mata Hari, Marlene Dietrich, James Bond or even Dracula riding along with them.

On the morning of our train ride, we put on our vintage outfits and caused a stir in the lobby of our hotel in Venice, The Bauer Palazzo, waiting to be picked up for our trip. When the boat arrived with its gleaming wood, we all boarded and the bellhops tagged our luggage. With the warm wind ruffling the plumes on our hats, and the light reflecting off the water, we were immediately swept into our own personal movie of sumptuous glamour and glitz.

111

We boarded the train to our adjoining cars, and were served champagne. We made our way to the Lalique car for a fancy 5-course lunch with tiny food surrounded by the luxurious art nouveau glass.

Then we returned to our cars to participate in my favorite train activity after meeting the other passengers: watching out the window.

We rumbled through sunny fields of wildflowers and rushing waterfalls. We passed through thunder and lightning, pouring rain, and storybook villages built into the sides of the mountains, a perfect reflection of our lives. We fell asleep that night watching *Top Hat* with Fred Astaire and Ginger Rogers, as the train chugged along, rocking us with its rumbling. The next morning we arrived in Paris and as we dragged our luggage through the dirty gray train station, a pink feather landed on my dress. I smiled, knowing the memories from this one night were a velvet bag full of glittering jewels I could open anytime I needed some magic… I just had to close my eyes.

The Orient Express

112

My Showgirl Pilgrimage to Josephine Baker's Castle

The first thing I did when I decided to tick some travel experiences off my bucket list, was reach into my dream file and pull out a folded up newspaper clipping about my hero, iconic showgirl Josephine Baker, and her castle in France. As I unfolded it for the hundredth time, I knew where I wanted to go.

When I was a teenager and first saw a black and white photo of Josephine staring out at me, dripping in jewels in a silk gown with her pet cheetah at her feet, my heart sang. She was everything I love about showgirls: glamorous, gorgeous, divinely decadent. I bought every book I could find about her. When I learned more about her life, she became my idol.

Now, I write mystery novels where my detective, Ellington Martini, is an ex-showgirl. In my new mystery novel, *The Champagne Scandal*, I wanted to delve deep into one of my favorite topics, burlesque costumes, and so I wrote a mystery that centers around the theft of some priceless costumes, namely Josephine Baker's tuxedo, jewels, and her banana skirt.

So really, my dream trip to Josephine's castle was not *just* a bucket list item, but research for my new book. Josephine's life was spectacular, and many times in the past two years, when I felt like I couldn't stand up, I would see her photo and remember her resilience. If Josephine could rise again and again, so could I.

Here are some of my favorite facts about Josephine:

1) She was born in Missouri, and worked as a domestic at the age of 8. She lived on the streets in a cardboard shelter, scavenging for food. Her first marriage was at age thirteen, and

she was married four times throughout her life. She became a professional performer at age fifteen, travelling to New York City, where she had moderate success in vaudeville and on Broadway, but when she went to Paris, she became a huge star.

2) She created the iconic banana dance, sang, and starred in movies. She also walked around Paris with her pet cheetah, Chiquita, who wore a diamond collar.

3) She bought her dream house, a medieval castle in the Dordogne Valley in France, and lived there for many years. It's called Chateau Des Milandes.

4) Her Rainbow Tribe: MY FAVORITE FACT about Josephine, the one that really hooked me, was that she adopted twelve children from twelve different countries because she wanted to show the world that hate is not inherent in human beings — it is taught — and that it is possible to live peacefully and joyfully.

5) She was a war hero: because she was a star, Josephine was able to move freely during the war — she carried secret messages to the troops hidden in her sheet music. She also used her castle as a place to hide soldiers.

6) When Josephine went broke because people took advantage of her generosity, she lost her castle, and who came to her rescue? Grace Kelly!

7) Grace Kelly adored Josephine. They had become friends at a NYC restaurant one night when the waiters refused to serve Josephine because she was black. Grace Kelly witnessed the way they treated Josephine and got up with her entire party and left. Josephine and Grace became friends, so when Josephine hit hard times, Princess Grace hired her to perform in Monaco and gave her a villa to live in, where she lived until her death in 1975.

8) Her final show was financed by Princess Grace and Jacquie O. She died four days later at age 68.

As you can see, Josephine was an extraordinary showgirl, a heroine, and someone to admire beyond her banana dance.

We stayed in a medieval village about thirty minutes from Josephine's castle. The road trip was stunning with picturesque castles, rolling green countryside, wide blue rivers, stone fences, and enchanting, ancient villages.

We parked in knee-high grass and walked up to Chateau Des Milandes, my hallowed ground. My heart was pounding like a jungle drum. Was I really here? Many people who visit the castle know nothing of Josephine. They come to see medieval history, or the "Birds of Prey" show, starring, falcons and owls. For me, walking on the path to the front door, I understood why Josephine had fallen in love with this place and chose to make her home here. I also understood her desire to save every child possible. I feel the same way.

The castle, or manor house, as the French call it, was a fort for hundreds of years. In 1489, Francois de Caumont built the castle as a wedding gift for his wife. In the 1930's, Josephine rented it and when it finally went up for sale in 1947, she bought it. Josephine poured her earnings into the castle and the entire town, installing electricity and water and bus shelters, as well as putting on performances that drew thousands of spectators. The current owners have tried to preserve the castle exactly as it was when Josephine lived there.

I walked in through the stone door and with each step, my heart sang, thinking that Josephine had walked this exact same floor many times. I walked through the costume room, filled with several of her stage costumes. For me, it was like visiting church, each costume a showgirl temple, each crystal sacred, each feather spiritual, each gown transformative. The climax was the glass box holding the banana skirt of course. To a non-showgirl eye, it looked like a heap of old fabric, but to me, it was like seeing the Holy Grail, and I expected a choir of angels to start singing when I saw it. I moved around the glass box, taking in every detail I could see, the stitching, the fabric, the shapes. The costumes had actually been found recently in an unopened trunk in the basement. Can you imagine opening an old steamer trunk in Josephine Baker's castle and finding her infamous banana skirt??? I didn't want to leave the bananas, but I reluctantly moved along to more rooms filled with incredible memorabilia, personal family photos, old programs and luxurious furniture. Many of her things had been sold off when the castle was taken from her. But her bedroom still had her canopy bed, and some chairs given to her as a wedding gift from a king (of course). There was a room with twelve cribs and rocking horses and the walls covered with photos of the children. The stairs were steep and curving, as medieval stairs are, and light filtered through ancient windows, illuminating the rooms. I looked out the small windows and imagined her looking out at her children running through the gardens, shouting and chasing butterflies.

I walked slowly savoring every feather and rhinestone, as my teenagers walked through the rooms at their own pace, much faster than mine. My daughter came up to me after a half hour and said, "When can we go?" I stared at her. "What? Why do you want to go?" She rolled her eyes. "I need to get back and lay out." I was too stunned to answer. Was my fifteen-year-old daughter really telling me we needed to leave my holy shrine so she could get a tan? Are you kidding me? Had she not heard one word I said? Had she not heard the build up to this day, the preparation and planning that went into this portion of the trip? Oh teenagers… can you really stand in a medieval castle and say you want to go back to the hotel and lay out? After I snapped out of my shock, I shook my head slowly and said, "I'm pretending this conversation did not happen. You know how important this is for me. Go sit outside in the sun and I'll be out when I'm ready." HONESTLY! I sighed and continued my exploration. I made my way through her castle, imagining her life there, her hopes and dreams and heartbreaks. Like me,

Josephine's husband ran off and left her, and still she didn't give up. She worked hard to support her twelve children as a single mom. When I finally made it to the last room before leaving the castle, I whispered, "Oh Josephine, I hope you know how truly extraordinary you were, and how your story still inspires so many people today."

Chez Josephine in NYC

The entire night at Chez Josephine was like being in a bubbly glass of glamour and glitz, glorious stories, sweeping music, and the beautiful haze that comes from being surrounded by images of iconic Josephine Baker, dear friends, raucous singing around a piano, and a splash of extra champagne.

It was midnight in NYC and I wasn't tired. I was standing in front of my billboard in Times Square with my sister and dear friends, Maria, Jennifer, and Dolphina. Dolphina suggested Chez Josephine. We walked over through the chaotic detritus of Times Square, and when I spotted the red velvet drapes and 1920's font, my heart started doing its own banana dance. We skipped across the street.

It lived up to its promise.

Walking through the front door was like entering another world. Red velvet drapes trimmed with golden tassels, brick walls covered with images of Josephine Baker at the height of her dancing, the kind of warm lighting that makes even the most weary of us look beautiful... Josephine peers out from every wall, bananas on her hips, feathers arching above her, body joyfully moving, her pet cheetah with a diamond collar walking beside her, a smile promising mischief...

Chez Josephine is everything I love about the 1920's, divine decadence, giddy and glamorous, an invitation to leave your cares outside and surrender to this one gorgeous moment. It was midnight, and there was only one other table occupied. I opened the menu and was swept away with all my favorite French wines and champagne. I sat down with my co-travelers, Dolphina, Jennifer, and my sister Maria.

A handsome man, Alberto, came over and asked if we'd like a drink. Being the responsible writer I am, I said just one glass of champagne, as I had my big book signing the next day and I was laser-focused.

He said he was having a special on bottles of Veuve.

I replied, "Definitely not. Dolphina and I are just having one glass and Maria and Jennifer don't even drink."

"Oh don't worry about that. I will give you the bottle to take back to your room. I'll even give you glasses to take with you."

My laser-focus promptly flew out the window.

I'm an easy sell when it comes to champagne.

My sister tells Alberto that this place is perfect for me, that I'm completely obsessed with Josephine Baker. She tells him that I wrote a mystery novel last year, and the main theft in the book was Josephine Baker's costumes. I chose Josephine as my subject because I wanted to spend time more time with her legacy, I wanted people to know how magnificent she was, and I wanted to visit her castle as "research," which I did in 2019.

Alberto said, "Well, her son is here. Do you want to meet him?"

Maria, Jennifer, and Dolphina all turn to stare at me, their mouths open.

"OMG! Her son? Her actual son? One of the Rainbow Tribe?"

He nods and sweeps our menus away as Maria smacks my arm. "Oh my gosh! This is meant to be! I can't believe it!"

Alberto, returned with a short blonde Frenchman named Jean-Claude, who looked at us suspiciously. My sister started to rave about my love for Josephine.

I nodded and placed a hand over my heart, gushing, "I am so inspired by her!"

He scowled at me and said something like, "My mother is my mother. It is natural, not extraordinary." When he said this, he karate-chopped the air with his hand.

But then he sat down, and had a glass of champagne, and then the stories started... he lived in the castle till he was 14. I told him I had visited the castle and he shrugged. I asked him about Monaco and Princess Grace and he told us how Prince Rainier and Grace Kelly invited them swimming, that Grace was a good friend of his mother's. Grace Kelly!

Jennifer, Dolphina, and my sister asked him heartfelt questions, while I sat quietly, barely able to contain the bubbles running up and down my body like a frothy glass of champagne. I couldn't believe I was sitting and talking to a member of the Rainbow Tribe.

My sister was delighted. She said, "Look at you! Swimming with Prince Rainer and Grace Kelly!"

He scowled and drank more champagne.

I pulled up a picture of the Rainbow Tribe on my phone and asked Jean Claude to show me which one was him. He pointed to the only blonde child. He was scowling as a child, the same way he was scowling now.

Eventually, Alfredo came over and turned the empty champagne bottle upside down to make sure there were no more drops.

Jean Claude graciously thanked us, bid us adieu, and left, and that's when I spotted the grand piano sitting in the middle of the room.

It just so happens that Jennifer was a rock star back in the 80's. She sat down and her fingers swept over the keys like long lost lovers, her dark hair falling over her face as she entered a meditative state particular to musicians who have found an instrument in an unexpected place. We started to sing, and I apologized to Alberto about our excessive volume, but he just waved a hand and said, "Sing as loud as you want!" At this point, we were the only ones left at Chez Josephine, and we let loose with some off-key glorious singing. I savored the moment, as I looked around at all the large-scale photos of Josephine surrounding me, the piano, the singing, the clinking glasses and the people I love next to me.

I didn't want to leave the hypnotic restaurant, but I will be back, soaking in the opulent red walls, maybe as a bestselling author, or a broke-ass author. Either way, I will be toasting Josephine.

Kindness on Airplanes

While most people I know hate traveling on planes, I love them. I love turning off my phone and being unreachable for a few hours. I love bringing a pile of books and trashy magazines, watching multiple movies, eating snacks, and having cold icy drinks delivered to me.

I have had my fair share of nasty travel experiences: long lines, dirty bathrooms, uncomfortable seats, cramped space, and people who seem to think they can conduct their personal hygiene routines in public. (I'm looking at you man who flosses his teeth on the plane and woman in yoga pants laying on the ground on her back breathing deeply in a full straddle.) Come on people!! There are certain things that should be done in private. Oy.

Aside from the nasty experiences, I have also met really fun people on planes like the Irish soccer team who drank too much, sang Irish songs, laughed uproariously, and in general made the plane trip feel like sitting at a really festive Irish pub. I sat in my seat and read my book, delighted by hearing all the fun they were having.

So lately, my life has taken a few hard left turns, leaving me reeling in grief. An airplane is the last place I would expect to find a moment of grace, and yet, I have had many experiences on planes with kindness, and I want to share two of them.

When I feel alone, or lost, I like to think about these moments because they give me hope for humanity and confirm for me what I already know — people can be really awesome.

Experience #1:

On the morning of October 27, 2018, I received a phone call. My dear friend Jen in LA said, "Can you talk?" and I happily said,

"Yes! I just made a cappuccino and I'm sitting down by the fire to write."

She said, "Okay," in her calm deep voice.

Then she took a deep breath and said, "She's still alive."

The ground dropped out from under me and my life changed forever for the worse as I shook my head, "No, no, no, no, no, no, no, no, no" each "no" louder and more desperate than the one before.

Jen told me that Kim had made herself stop breathing. The paramedics were able to restart her heart twice on the way to the hospital, and she was now on a ventilator while they froze her body to see if they could bring her back. My friends said, "Go. We've got the kids." I packed and got on my flight.

All these years, I had loved catapulting through the air in the safe metal egg-shaped planes, but now I felt like I'd been thrown out the window and was catapulting through the air with no parachute.

I boarded Delta and sat in my seat staring at the screen with nothing on it.

The airline attendant chirped, "Are you going to LA for business or pleasure?"

In shock, I said, "Neither. My best friend tried to kill herself and is in a coma and I am going to the hospital."

Her eyes welled with tears. She put her hand on my shoulder and squeezed and said softly, "I'm so sorry." She brought me a blanket and tucked it around me.

A few minutes later, another airline attendant came and knelt next to my seat in the aisle. She said, "Hey, I heard what happened. I understand. I went through something similar. My brother is Bipolar. Please let me know if there's anything I can do." She hugged me. Another attendant brought me extra cookies as I sat staring straight ahead. When I exited the plane, they all stood at the door and hugged me with tears in their eyes. Their kindness and compassion were soft lanterns as I headed out the door to face the darkest night of my life.

Experience #2

A month later, I was flying back from Kim's memorial with my kids and my Mom. You probably think you know how tiny and disgusting airplane bathrooms are, but you don't really, not until you have flown with an elderly woman with painful swollen feet and dementia who keeps peeing her pants and you have to change her on a crowded plane. It suddenly occurred to me there must be a large bathroom somewhere on airplanes. What would you do if you had a wheelchair? I'm not sure where I thought an airplane would hide a large bathroom, but I asked the airline attendant who laughed and shook her head.

My Mom didn't want to get up, but I didn't want her sitting in a wet diaper for six hours. "Come on, Mom." I said with a huge smile, the kind of smile I give to a frightened child to reassure them. I walked backwards down the aisle, facing her, encouraging her to follow me with the weird big smile on my face, thinking, "How in the hell did we get here? My beautiful Kim, gone; my beautiful Mom, lost without my Dad, and me, leading her down an airplane aisle to change her.

The airline attendants didn't know what to do about changing my mom, although I have to imagine I'm not the first person on the planet to travel with an incontinent elderly person. We both couldn't fit in the bathroom, and the airline attendant told me I couldn't change her outside the bathroom.

"What am I supposed to do? What do other people do?"

She shrugged, her eyes big.

I said, "I'm changing her, even if it means standing in the

middle of the aisle."

Finally, the airline attendant held up a coat as a curtain, while I helped my mom change as quickly as possible. As I kneeled in the back of that plane, directing my mom to lift one swollen foot at a time while she stared at me in confusion.

I thought, "Really life? REALLY?"

I stood up feeling like I'd just run a marathon, quickly washed my hands, and led her back to our seats, the same giant smile on my face. She stared at me, confused, and hobbled along not sure what we were doing or where we were, but I looked familiar to her so she followed me. I got her tucked back into her seat next to the kids, who stood up and helped get her buckled and situated, and finally collapsed into my own seat across the aisle.

I lifted my bottle of water to my mouth, feeling like I was going to throw up, my hand shaking badly, but that was normal for me after all the loss.

A few minutes later, a woman two rows behind me dropped a note on my tray, written on a vomit bag. It said:

My Mother had dementia for years. I'm not sure if your mother does, but she reminds me of my mom. I know how hard it is, but you are doing an amazing job. Your mother is lucky to have you. Wishing you strength and peace. Happy Holidays!

This random act of kindness from a stranger made me cry, and I still cry every time I read it. I turned and smiled at her, putting my hand on my heart and mouthing the words "Thank you". She nodded and went back to her book, and I felt a tiny bit lighter, almost like I was wearing a parachute.

Look for the Rainbows

On a typical Spring Break, I would take my kids to see family. On Spring Break 2018, we were reeling in grief, and the Muir Woods popped into my head. I felt like it would be healing to all of us to walk in an ancient forest among the redwoods.

I was trying to follow my instinct and do the things I felt compelled to do, even if I didn't know why. My inner core was compelling me to Northern California, and coincidentally that's where my old backpacking partners live: Zar and Tanya. I hadn't seen them in years, but we spoke occasionally and I knew they were both mothers but other than that, they hadn't changed at all since our traveling days.

We went to wine country on my birthday with Zar and Tanya and the kids. And as we drove through the gorgeous vineyards, we saw not one, not two, but SEVEN RAINBOWS! SEVEN!!!!

It seemed like a personal message to me, from my Dad, or the universe, or the whomever it is that makes rainbows, that everything was going to be okay, even though I couldn't imagine how.

I had not seen a rainbow at this point in about fifteen years.

Here I was, on my 49th birthday, finally seeing a sky full of rainbows again. I was screaming in the car and yelling for Zar to pull over so I could take a picture.

Annabelle said, "Mom, stop screaming, you're scaring Zar and Tanya." I tried to tone it down, but I was high on rainbows! Okay, I guess I'll admit I get a little over-excited when I see a rainbow.

Later, I told my friend Courtney about the day, and asked her if it was extraordinary that I screamed when I saw a rainbow like someone else might scream seeing Mick Jagger.

She quietly said, "Maybe."

I said, "Well, what do you do when you see rainbows?"

She said, "I might smile to myself, I might take a picture, but I don't scream and jump up and down."

Hmmm, okay.

So maybe I was overreacting, but I truly madly deeply love rainbows.

The next day we went to the Muir Woods, and guess what?

We saw so many more rainbows. They were shooting everywhere through the woods. They were shooting off the kids like cat whiskers, shooting through the trees, dancing in my hair like jewels.

Everything in that forest looked like it was glowing and unfurling and wrapping me in beauty.

It was like an acid flashback—if I had ever done acid—which I haven't—but I imagine it would be like this—the glowing colors, the furling fronds, the flowers looked like they were blooming right in front of my eyes--it was that powerful.

I had my Rumi book of poetry with me, and I read lines of poetry while we walked among these massive gorgeous trees, the smell of redwood and moss everywhere, neon green ferns gracefully waving at our feet, and I thought, "I don't need a house, I could live right here next to these magnificent trees and be very happy."

AND

we saw ANOTHER RAINBOW the next day.

This one was like a massive waterfall rainbow pouting through the rainclouds in such vibrant colors—it was the first time I had seen the purple in a rainbow so thick and bright.

We were on a quest to see the Jules Feiffer waterfall in Big Sur, as waterfalls are another thing that heals my soul. We drove a long way on winding roads above steep ocean cliffs, surrounded by one of my favorite smells — pine trees and ocean mixed together. We got to the waterfall and hiked down the path, and looked with excitement, only to find the waterfall was a small trickle. The kids were exasperated with my quest to see the trickle, but the magic was in the journey, and after the trip was over, Annabelle said it was her favorite part. She loved driving through the dark in the rain on ocean cliffs, through farmlands, listening to Nancy Drew on audio book while the rain pelted our car — after seeing the massive rainbow of course.

And rainbows and waterfalls and poetry are all things that heal me, but the best part was spending time with Zar and Tanya and Annabelle and Henry, creating memories that can never be taken away, no matter what we go through in life.

And when we came home, I decided to start teaching a Rainbow Unicorn class at my kids school as an after-school class, which became so popular that it's now my summer camp and I'm still teaching it. The kids and I show up in glitter rainbow clothing. I can completely indulge my overenthusiasm for rainbows and all things magical with tiny humans who share my enthusiasm.

I hope my kids take away that when we need support, it's all around us, in the people we love, in the trees and the sea, in waterfalls and rainbows — we just have to open our eyes.

Kiki de Montparnasse in NYC

I was fascinated by Kiki long before her name was used on a high end lingerie store. She was a popular artist's model back in the 1920's, with adorable bangs and short black flapper hair. She was a muse for famous photographer Man Ray, and you have more than likely seen her image somewhere.

So I had heard about the new line of lingerie shops, and I was visiting NYC when I saw Kiki de Montparnasse on the street in Soho. I entered its sleek black interior to see if any treasures awaited me. The entire lingerie line was a little too streamlined and glossy for my taste, so I was just about to leave when I spotted something fluffy in a display case. My heart started to skip as it does when I spot something meant for me, and I took a closer look. It was two tufts of ostrich feathers, one black, one white, attached to an iron ring. I asked to see them, slipped them on my fingers, and proceeded to strut around the store, waving my hands in the air like I was talking, putting my be-feathered hands on my hips, and in general, making an extravagant show of the enormous feathered rings. I thought how wonderfully creative to put a tuft of feathers on a ring! I imagined how whimsical and glamorous I would look, walking around Soho with enormous, but light and floaty feathered rings. How brilliant! I asked the salesgirl, "How much?" She answered, "$15."

"Oh my god, I'll take both," I said, delighted by the fact I was leaving this very expensive shop with the cutest items in there for less than $40. The salesgirl was very excited. She ran in the back and came back with two velvet boxes lined in satin for my new rings. While she was rummaging for something, I looked at the box. It didn't say, "$15.00." It said, "$1,500.00."

Darling salesgirl! $15 is very different from $15 hundred! I sadly parted with my rings, laying them on the counter. "I've decided to think about it," I said politely, backing out of the store as quickly as possible. Later on, I posted the story and a male friend said, "Marci, I don't think those rings were meant for your fingers."

Oh my. My face turned bright red as I realized my error. Of course misshapen iron rings in a lingerie store aren't meant for your fingers!! What was I thinking? Why oh why didn't the salesgirl gently inform me that they were meant for a different body part?

In the end, at least I can laugh about it. And it has given me an idea, I wonder if rings with tufts of feathers might be a new style item? I wonder if anyone would wear them? OR would they find other places on their bodies to adorn?

Where It All Started: Road Tripping with My Mom and Dad

My Dad LOVED to road trip, and I grew up spending a lot of time in the backseat, looking out the window of the car. I can still see flashes of the miles of empty road, and then the appearance of a lone cabin in a massive green field during a lightning storm; looming mountains; red rock cliffs, redwoods as tall as a skyscraper; canyons in swirling reds, golds, and white streaks…

We sang songs and listened to stories in the car. My Mom's favorite car story was Dracula, and she loved to imitate the panting of Van Helsing as he ran around trying to get rid of the monster. We listened to Dracula on dark stormy car rides, my Mom hooking her arm in my Dad's arm, scooting closer to him on the scary parts, leaning over to kiss his cheek or nuzzle his ear.

After he died, she told me that when he took her on their first date at the drive-in movie back in 1957, he was a gentleman and stayed on his side of the front seat. She really wanted him to kiss her, so she finally leaned over to kiss him on the cheek. Her face glowed when she described how he whipped his arm around her and pulled her close to him. And forever after that, he called her his "Hot Tamale."

Now he's gone and her mind is gone and she no longer remembers him.

My Dad loved storytelling music, and we listened to his favorites in the car, so we knew every word of nearly every song by Marty Robbins and Kenny Rogers. My Dad loved any song that brought a tear to his eye or made him laugh, like the "Cattle Call" by Slim Whitman with all of it's yodeling. Even today, when I hear Roger Whitaker's velvety voice, I am slammed back into the back seat of the car, my window down, my hair whipped around by a warm desert wind.

We drove all over Utah and California, often driving hours out of the way so he could see the ruins of a pioneer cemetery or a ghost town. We would pull over on the dirt road, park, and walk around, looking for clues of who had lived there.

We took little trips and epic road trips, once driving from Canada down the entire winding coast to southern California. We stopped at flower gardens, redwood forests, ocean views, and chocolate factories. We sang songs, talked for hours, and spent a lot of time looking out the window.

Many years later, I was considering shipping my car from New Orleans to Boston as we were moving and I didn't want my young children to have to sit in the car for three days. My parents volunteered to drive it, so they flew to New Orleans. I decided I could not fly home with my kids while my parents took an epic road trip without me. I cancelled our flights and we all piled into the car, not knowing it would be the most incredible road trip of our lives.

I drove, and my parents took turns riding in front. We followed the map, my Dad as navigator, neatly folding the map on the dashboard and marking our path with a pen. The kids sat in their car seats, wearing head phones and listening to Harry Potter on tape which kept them enrapt for most of the trip.

We ended up off the usual course because there was a hurricane moving up the coast. That's how we ended up in Gettysburg. My parents love history, and Gettysburg was something they had always wanted to see. We stayed in a 300-year old tavern and took Civil War tours. We toured the house where Abraham Lincoln slept the night the day before he gave the Gettysburg Address. My Dad had tears in his eyes as we stood on a hill overlooking the battlefields. You could almost hear the musket shots and clink of swords.

When we left Gettysburg, my Mom decided she wanted to a real handmade Amish doll, so we drove hours out of our way to find an authentic Amish town. She had stars in her eyes as she ran her hands over the quilts and little dolls, until she picked one up and saw the tag that said it was made in a different country.

When we finally made it to Boston, we ended up staying in a haunted hotel in Salem. It's been nearly ten years since that road trip, and my children still talk about it. They remember how quiet the car was before we stopped for coffee, and after coffee, how the entire car hopped with our jubilant singing and car-dancing. They still remember the important life skills my Dad taught them on that trip, like hanging spoons off their noses. And they still talk about eating at a tavern in Gettysburg, playing on the warm sidewalk at twilight, watching my parents nuzzle each other and slow dance as the sun set.

I hope that's what my Mom and Dad are doing now wherever they are. I like to imagine they are forever locked in each other's embrace, slow dancing in a pink sky--that would be heaven for them.

And for now, I will continue taking my children on road trips, and having them tell me their favorite memories of our past journeys, so they don't forget and will have a bag full of stories of their own.

Kim: My Magnificent Merchant of Marvels

*Note: I did not speak at Kim's memorial because I was holding my sobbing son. If I had spoken, this is what I would have said.

From swimming in waterfalls amid ancient ruins in Mexico; to fairy hunting and chasing rainbows on the Isle of Skye... To falling asleep on each other's shoulders in Westminster Abbey to taking wicked tours in Charleston; From riding around Manhattan in a limo wearing shoes that glowed in the dark to running through the woods of Martha's Vineyard; from swinging on chandeliers in Palm Springs (literally) to sitting on our swing in the backyard of the Royal Palace, wearing our flower crowns; Kim was my twin soul, my partner in crime, my truest love.

Kim had many names: Rocket Sapphire, Vermilion, Rocket Larkspur, and Lucky Murphy. I always called her my Merchant of Marvels and she called me her Monarch of Magic. Together we sailed on a Ship of Dreams.

I didn't just meet Kim, I recognized her.

We met when we both played fairies in Midsummer Night's Dream at The Globe in West Hollywood. Our souls clicked. I distinctly remember lying in the fairy bower next to her, me as Peasblossom, she as Mustardseed. She was singing the Fairy Queen to sleep in her bold clear voice, and I closed my eyes and let the warm nest of her voice surround me.

On our first outing together outside the theater, I invited her to a coffee shop called Highland Grounds where my friend, Chuck E. Weiss, played New Orleans blues every Sunday night. I wore a long red cotton dress and braids in my hair. We were sitting at the counter, the music pouring over us, when Chuck E.'s long time friend, Tom Waits, walked in and sat down next to us. We spent the night talking to him and listening to Chuck E. Because I was completely enamored of Tom's music at the time, I thought of Kim as my good luck charm. The next day I invited her to go on my daily roller-skating trip around the Hollywood Reservoir. We talked about rainbows and sunshine and beauty, and when I dropped her back at her apartment in Hollywood, I shouted, "I love my life!" Later she told me that comment had stopped her in her tracks. She had never heard anyone say that before and she wanted to love her life too.

We were inseparable after that. Everyone else disappeared when we were together. We eventually moved into the Royal Palace, and even though some might have viewed our little duplex in a sketchy neighborhood as non-magical, to us, we lived like royalty because we were together.

It was like life bloomed into luminous magic when we were together. We gave ourselves royal names. She called herself Empress Genevieve and I called myself Princess Selena Delaluna after the moon goddess. All visitors to our home came up with their own royal names, from Countess Valerie to Princess Farhana. We couldn't believe our luck to have found a home in LA in our budget, that had roses and honeysuckle blooming everywhere, drenching the air with their sweet scent. We had our very own orange tree, and every year on Kim's birthday in February, the massive jasmine covering our house bloomed. Every birthday evening, I cut the vines and made her a jasmine crown.

We decided to paint every room a different color. My room was pink with a blue sky and clouds overhead Kim's was painted to look like a circus tent, our bathroom was the aquarium, and that back room was our "opium room," painted cabernet red and filled with our costumes. Kim created a magical invitation

135

to our housewarming party. She drew and cut out large keys and tied them with a ribbon, sending them out to our friends. We thought ourselves hilarious when we decided to add, "Prize given for best housewarming gift."

I remember that party vividly, forty people sitting on the grass in our tiny backyard, watching the deck, which we were using as a stage. Because all our friends were performers, our parties became epic talent shows. Veena and Neena performed a gorgeous Indian dance that ended with them throwing colorful flowers over the audience. Mohammed Khordadian performed his masterful Persian folk dances, Dolphina did a pirate dance, and Kim and I performed the final number, an improvised dance to "Our House" by Crosby Stills and Nash. I still remember feeling like we were wrapped in a warm cloud of love as we danced together.

Kim and I both adored make believe. We loved to pretend we were sailing on a magical ship through warm starry skies, and even now, that she's gone, I think of her as Captain of her own ship with a rainbow sail. We used to drive down the freeway in LA at night in my convertible VW bug with the top down, and she'd sit high in the passenger seat holding my rainbow silk veil up like a sail, and we'd play ethereal music and sing and pretend we were sailing through the sky, giggling and whooping and trying not to lose the veil in the warm whipping wind.

Kim designed her bedroom with patchwork drapes and a loft bed with wavy sides. She covered her bed in crimson and purple velvet. I had a velvet bag made for her in the same colors with patchwork stars on it. She filled it with glitter that she could give away.

In the books Harry Potter, JK Rowling created the "Dementors" as a metaphor for depression. If you get kissed by a Dementor, they suck all hope out of you and you are in a prison of darkness. The darkest day of my life was the day the Dementors got to my magnificent Merchant of Marvels.

Kim took her own life in 2018.

In my thoughts, Kim is still wearing her red velvet sorcerer's hat, of course, and her velvet bag with patchwork stars. She climbs back aboard the Ship of Dreams, of which she is captain of course. The sail is billowing rainbow silk with star-shaped patches. The sky is warm and her velvet bag is full of actual stars that she can throw out into the sky whenever she wants. Dear Kim, I'll be looking up, my eyes open wide, my heart open wide, my arms open wide, ready to catch them.

Gratitude List

Thank you to my traveling partners in crime: Kim, Zar, Tanya, Eric, Marlise, Maria, Rogelio, Courtney, and all the people I met along the way...

Cheers and gratitude to all the women in Girls Love Travel who responded so positively and passionately to my tales and made me realize there were people out there who actually might want to hear my travel stories.

Thank you to Leslie Zemeckis, for being my favorite Barbie cheerleader. Next time we are in Paris, champagne is on me!

Thank you Annabelle and Henry, my hearts.

Thank you to my Dad, for teaching me to follow my own path and cheering me every step of the way.

And thank you to Kim, my queen... the sea still shimmers with reflections of our moonlit balls.

In my dress of Starlight, Venice

About the Author:

Marci Darling is the author of three bestselling books: Martini Mystery: A Love Letter to New Orleans; The Champagne Scandal: The Spirits Are Calling; and Divorce Diva: Navigating Grief and Loss with Hope, Humor, and Chutzpah. In addition to her writing career, Marci worked as a professional belly dancer for more than a decade and danced on tour with The Go-Go's, B-52's, and Paul McCartney. She has a Masters from Harvard, a BA from UCLA, and a Certificate in Novel Writing from Stanford. She is a member of Mystery Writers of America and a Founding Member of the Martini Club. She lives in a cottage by the sea with her two children, two hooligan dogs, two cats, and one Ewok in disguise as a cat.